REBURYING THE PAST: THE EFFECTS OF REPATRIATION AND REBURIAL ON SCIENTIFIC INQUIRY

REBURYING THE PAST: THE EFFECTS OF REPATRIATION AND REBURIAL ON SCIENTIFIC INQUIRY

ELIZABETH WEISS

Nova Science Publishers, Inc.
New York

NOTICE TO THE READER

The Publisher has taken reasonable care in the preparation of this book, but makes no expressed or implied warranty of any kind and assumes no responsibility for any errors or omissions. No liability is assumed for incidental or consequential damages in connection with or arising out of information contained in this book. The Publisher shall not be liable for any special, consequential, or exemplary damages resulting, in whole or in part, from the readers' use of, or reliance upon, this material. Any parts of this book based on government reports are so indicated and copyright is claimed for those parts to the extent applicable to compilations of such works.

Independent verification should be sought for any data, advice or recommendations contained in this book. In addition, no responsibility is assumed by the publisher for any injury and/or damage to persons or property arising from any methods, products, instructions, ideas or otherwise contained in this publication.

This publication is designed to provide accurate and authoritative information with regard to the subject matter covered herein. It is sold with the clear understanding that the Publisher is not engaged in rendering legal or any other professional services. If legal or any other expert assistance is required, the services of a competent person should be sought. FROM A DECLARATION OF PARTICIPANTS JOINTLY ADOPTED BY A COMMITTEE OF THE AMERICAN BAR ASSOCIATION AND A COMMITTEE OF PUBLISHERS.

LIBRARY OF CONGRESS CATALOGING-IN-PUBLICATION DATA
Weiss, Elizabeth.
Reburying the past : the effects of repatriation and reburial on scientific inquiry / Elizabeth Weiss (author).   p. cm.
Includes bibliographical references and index.
ISBN 978-1-60456-701-4 (hardcover : alk. paper)
1. Human remains (Archaeology)--Repatriation. 2. Archaeology--Moral and ethical aspects. 3. Archaeology--Law and legislation. 4. Archaeology--Political aspects. I. Title.
CC79.5.H85W45 2009
930.1--dc22   2008023064

Published by Nova Science Publishers, Inc. ≃ New York

CONTENTS

PREFACE

In this new book, the author puts forth what one can learn from the study of human remains, how human remains have been obtained, the ethical dilemmas surrounding working with human remains, and the legal and political complexities of repatriation and reburial. The author intends to introduce readers to a fascinating realm of science rarely covered in the media, as opposed to the more popular fields of anthropology (e.g. forensics, archaeology, paleoanthropology).

ACKNOWLEDGEMENTS

I would like to first thank my parents Gisela and David. They raised me to think critically, form strong morals, and not be afraid to share my thoughts. Without their help, I could not have come this far. I would like to extend my thanks to my siblings, Katherine, Alex, and Chris who have motivated me and kept me on my toes. In a family of successful siblings and a competitive nature, you never rest on your laurels. My aunt Claire-Lise Holy inspired me by being a strong role model who has shown me that you can love your work and still have a rich life outside of work. A thanks also goes to Don Dias for his continuous support and belief in my ability to accomplish this goal.

There are many people who have supported me at my university; the College of Social Sciences at San Jose State University provided me with the release time to complete this work. Also, the college supported endeavors to discover the changes NAGPRA has caused in anthropology. The Department of Anthropology's current Chair, Dr. Chuck Darrah, and the past Chair, Dr. Jan English-Lueck, have been supportive as well and have never cast doubt on my ambitions or morals.

I am also very grateful to those anthropologists and lawyers who read earlier works and encouraged my continuous struggle in understanding the causes and effects of reburial on anthropology, some of these individuals include Dr. Gary Huckleberry, Attorney Jerry Springer, and Dr. Tom Layton. Many more have provided feedback and encouragement; I wish that I could list them all.

I am grateful to Nova Science Publishers who were brave enough to publish this work. Finally, I would like to thank the students at San Jose State University (with a special thanks to Beth Mabie and Cathy Mistely); students are our future and they make my job rewarding and promising.

Chapter 1

INTRODUCTION

"As scientists, it is our ethical obligation to study and try to explain the world around us. NAGPRA and other repatriation laws obstruct the process of scientific endeavors; thereby, creating an ethical dilemma for scientists."

Elizabeth Weiss (2006: Research & NAGPRA.
Society for American Archaeology Archaeological Record Vol. 6).

Sitting in a room with anthropologists and Native Americans at a conference concerning NAGPRA (Native American Graves Protection and Repatriation Act) compliance in a San Francisco hotel, I feel immediately like the outsider. We are there to discuss issues surrounding repatriation and reburial laws in regards to the skeletal collections housed within California's largest public university system, California State Universities. Repatriation refers to the act of giving skeletal remains of past peoples to related modern peoples; reburial is the act of burying these skeletal remains. There are representatives from most of the universities in the California State Universities system and I am there with the former Chair of my department from San Jose State University. San Jose State University, which is the oldest university in the California State Universities system, houses one of the largest single population prehistoric skeletal collections in the United States. This collection consists of nearly 300 individuals and used to be nearly triple that size before the reburial of the other part of the collection by Stanford University and the Native American tribe of the Muwekma-Ohlone (also referred to as the Ohlone-Costanoans) who claim to be descendents of the skeletal population housed at San Jose State University.

The meeting begins calmly with introduction of names and other pertinent information. I am a physical anthropologist with a specialty in the study of human remains from the archaeological record. Sometimes people will call those who study these remains bioarchaeologists or osteologists. My career is devoted to reconstructing past lives using skeletal remains and I feel a great deal of respect for the knowledge that can be gleaned from these individuals. Others in the room range from physical anthropologists to cultural anthropologists (who study living populations and their cultures, such as what they eat, their religions, family make-up, etc.) to Native Americans. As soon as the niceties were over, we dove into the realm of repatriation and reburial laws, which are federal and state laws that affect any government funded agency (including universities) holding human remains and artifacts.

Although academics are supposedly taught to be objective, the first speaker and the host of the conference starts with an emotional ploy to tug at our moral heartstrings. He tells of his walk up to a veteran cemetery and looking down at the city on the Bay, San Francisco, where there are prehistoric human remains that were recovered from construction sites and he ties this into how he would feel if his own grandfather, who is buried at the veteran cemetery would be dug up and studied. With tears in his eyes, he tells story after story of human remains that have been found and studied. He emphasizes the need to be sensitive and put ourselves in the Native American minds. However, my eyes stay dry.

I was right, I didn't fit in and as the meeting wore on and more teary-eyed academics and Native Americans spoke, the more I realized that I was not in friendly territory. Towards the end of the conference after having been bombarded with other peoples' morality, I was feeling exhausted. The breaking point came when one of the Native American women said she thought it was important that us academics treat the human remains with respect. I had had enough; I spoke up and, thus, escalated other peoples' emotions from condescension into furor. I said that it was important to assume that we all would be respectful rather than assume that we would not be. Weren't we innocent until proven guilty? No, we were guilty for the sins of others; those anthropologists of the past who studied race differences, the Europeans who came and took the land, and any other historical group who displaced minorities. I realized this when another Native American spoke up and said that I didn't know how it felt to be a victim and, therefore, shouldn't be voicing my opinion. According to them, I did not come from an oppressed or victimized social group. An anthropologist then spoke the unthinkable comparing me to a Nazi while tears were running down her cheeks. She said she never wanted to touch another skeleton in her life. By now at least four people were crying and upset and the fact that I had pointed out my half-Jewish and half-German ancestry made little difference. Was I supposed to feel guilty for my German side and victimized for my Jewish? The conference ended with no one shaking my hand, some not even being able to look at me, and a few being down right rude. So, I thought, where do I fit in?

I have no compunction to feel the morality that the others felt, which is not to say that I am immoral or even amoral. Quite the contrary, my passion lies with telling the story of these past peoples in an accurate manner. My ethics are entrenched in the scientist's duty, which is to study the world around us and explain it to the best of our ability, to discover truths and realize when past truths need to be replaced due to new scientific discoveries. Cultural anthropologists often evoke cultural relativity to help us understand and tolerate those who are different from ourselves, but this relativity is not always extended to Western culture. Cultural relativity is a theory suggesting that what is good and bad can be relative; for example, whether you bury human remains or cremate them is a matter of your culture and one is just as good as the other. I ask you to keep cultural relativity in mind when you read this book; not everyone has spirituality, not everyone believes in God or an afterlife. Some come from cultures steeped in scientific endeavors and a desire to ask and answer questions without faith clouding up the answers. This is where I fit in.

How would I feel if my grandfather was unburied and studied? I would feel proud that his skeletal remains were still of use. I have suggested to my own parents to donate their bodies after their deaths to science and I plan to do so myself. Moreover, many European cultures have an intriguing interest in anatomy, display of remains, and pride in skeletal remains found in their countries. To think that the only response could be that everyone wants their ancestors, or even relatives, to be buried or cremated is a total lack of cultural relativity in practice. Anatomical displays, such as BodyWorlds, hail from Europe and have a long history there (think of Leonardo da Vinci and the catacombs). Egyptians, as well, have a strong pride in the display of their mummy collections of the Pharaohs and other ancient Egyptians, with many Egyptians claiming a direct ancestry to these past peoples.

Hence, I want to take you into a world where human skeletal remains are not "probed and prodded," for a scientist's weird lab test as Mark MacKinnon, a reporter for Canada's *Globe and Mail* newspaper, suggested in his August 2000 article. But, rather a sophisticated science that helps us tell the real story of how these past people lived and died. Bioarchaeologists have a strong respect for human remains, which stems from their love of anatomy, the desire to speak for those who cannot speak, and the ethos of science. The anti-scientific bias inherent in the reporting of repatriations is abundant, not only in the Canadian article, but here in the US, where *Time* authors Jeffrey Kluger and Dan Cray bemoan the ill-will that has occurred due to the Kennewick Man case (a 9,300 year-old skeleton that scientists fought for and Native Americans wanted reburied). One example comes from Kluger and Cray's quote regarding reburial in Nebraska: "After decades of watching researchers plunder its burial grounds for bodies and artifacts, the tribe finally forced Nebraska researchers and museums to return the items in 1989."

In this book, you will find a discussion of bioarchaeological science that is rarely covered by the media. I will show you that modern scientists are not just interested in race, seeking to define who is superior to whom, and drawing family trees. I will try to convince you that anthropologists are not grave robbers, but rather the ones who have salvaged thousands of human remains that were on the brink of being crushed by the process of construction. The regulations in place to repatriate and rebury the remains will be outlined along with the complications that arise from these laws. Then, how does this affect our science and our knowledge of the past? Can we still have bioarchaeology without human remains? I will also address ethical dilemmas from Native American perspectives in conjunction with religious causes and scientists' views.

Chapter 2

WHY STUDY HUMAN REMAINS?

"In my view, archaeologists have a responsibility to the people they study. They are defining the culture of an extinct group and in presenting their research they are writing a chapter of human history that cannot be written except from archaeological investigation. If the archaeology is not done, the ancient people remain without a history."

Clement W. Meighan (1993: Burying American Archaeology,
Academic Questions Vol. 6).

WHAT ONE CAN LEARN FROM STUDYING HUMAN REMAINS

In the 2001 book *The Future of the Past*, anthropologist Dr. Brenda Baker at Arizona State Museum and University along with several of her colleagues states precisely why we, anthropologists, study human remains:

"Physical anthropologists today seek the benefits of studying remains of past peoples, not just for anthropologists or for Native Americans, but for society as a whole."

It may be already obvious to you that I have a strong passion for the preservation of human remains, but you may be wondering where this passion arises from; that is, why make a career out of studying prehistoric populations? As I started my college education in anthropology, I wanted to pursue a career focused on human evolution. My desire was to learn about our earliest ancestors and what led them to evolve eventually into modern humans. I was fascinated with the field of paleoanthropology, which is the study of human evolution through the fossil record. How then did I get to become an expert in these much more recent remains? As I entered graduate school, it became clear that any thesis research would need to be conducted on remains that were readily available, which happened to be California prehistoric Indian remains. I conducted my Master's research on sex differences in the lower limb with the viewpoint that these skills could still be transferred to human evolutionary studies. But, as an actor gets typecast, I got typecast as a student of Amerind (American Indian) studies and was handed one great opportunity after another. Since my study of 9,300 year-old Kennewick Man's thigh and shin, I have never returned to human evolutionary studies.

I never regretted the course my career has taken. Bioarchaeology has some advantages over paleoanthropology and the questions that need to be asked in bioarchaeology are as fascinating as those in human evolutionary studies. Early bioarchaeologists were similar to paleoanthropologists because the sample sizes that were studied were extremely small. As a result, early bioarchaeology was filled with case studies and descriptive works. Since the development of the Western world (and specifically the United States) large samples have been the rule rather than the exception in bioarchaeological studies. What does this mean for anthropologists? It means that we can perform rigorous scientific research that is based on answering questions rather than just describing the human remains. These questions are answered using statistics that help us determine whether similarities and differences examined are more than just chance. Through the scientific study of human remains, which has only just begun in the last forty years, a plethora of research has emerged to help us reconstruct the lives of the earliest Americans.

RECONSTRUCTING PAST LIVES: BRINGING THE DEAD BACK TO LIFE

One of the most controversial topics in bioarchaeology is that of the peopling of the Americas. Early anthropologists had set a late date for the arrival of modern humans in the New World. For most of the field's history, 13,000 to 15,000 years ago had been the standard date for Amerinds crossing the Bering Land Bridge and entering North America. This coincided neatly with the climatic changes that were occurring at the time and fit well with the anatomy of modern American Indians, which appear to have Asian ancestry with a cold-adapted physique. For example, cold adapted individuals tend to have shorter distal elements (such as forearms compared to upper arms as well as short fingers) to avoid frostbite and conserve heat. We see this morphology (or body shape) in Asians and modern Native Americans.

Conversely, more recent finds of older skeletal remains and artifacts have been causing anthropologists to question this version of early North American prehistory. One piece of the evidence that has been used to contradict this hypothesis is that the earliest tools and remains are not found far north, but rather fairly far south (in Chile, for example), which means that either the Amerinds arrived earlier through the north passage or that they used a different route. Another piece of evidence that suggests that the Bering Land Strait hypothesis may be faulty comes from our earliest Amerind skeletal remains. These Paleo-Indians, such as the 9,300 year-old Kennewick Man (found in Washington state), the 8,400 year-old Spirit Cave Man (found in Nevada), the 12,000 year-old Lucia (found in Brazil), plus remains from Florida that date back to 10,000 years, do not look like modern Native Americans. Some of these individuals have yet to have the cold adapted morphology of the Native Americans occupying the Americas later in prehistory and presently. These features, which are present in modern Native Americans, include wide-heads, broad bodies with relatively short distal elements (as mentioned above) and pronounced cheekbones. More interestingly, these Paleo-Indians do not appear similar to each other either. Some of them look like Australian Aborigines while others look more like they would have been Ainu (the Native Japanese population that are very Caucasian in appearance).

What this early Paleo-Indian diversity suggests is that there were many migrations into the Americas, which shouldn't be surprising considering that the movement of early humans out of Africa consisted of many migrations and we still see waves of migrations today all over the world. The likelihood that in prehistory there was only one migration into the New World is extremely slim; this is not what we ever see in the fossil record, in animal migrations, and in modern human behavior. This hypothesis of multiple migrations is controversial because it suggests that modern Native Americans replaced Paleo-Indians and, therefore, Native Americans are no better than the later Europeans who "stole their land." Furthermore, if the Paleo-Indians have been replaced by later groups, then modern Native Americans should have no more claims to their remains than modern Europeans.

Native Americans often present their creation myths as armor against the scientific evidence emerging in the new hypothesis of the peopling of the Americas. For example, in the Kennewick Man case, the tribe of American Indians who tried to claim the 9,300 year-old skeleton did so on the basis of their creation myth. Like many other Native Americans, the Umatilla's creation myth could be paraphrased as "we know that our people have been part of this land from the beginning of time." As journalist Douglas Preston astutely pointed out in his 1997 article for the *New Yorker*, they did not want scientists to contradict their myths and were especially motivated to rebury Kennewick Man given his alleged Caucasoid features and the publicity this had generated. Interestingly, Native Americans were initially glad to hear about the possibility of their early arrival in the Americas. They thought that this would help their NAGPRA claims, but little did they expect what would follow. The scientific data seemed to suggest that these earliest Americans were from a different ancestry as the later arrivals. Consequently, the modern Native Americans replaced earlier ones. After all, skeletons such as Kennewick Man might be used to suggest that modern Native Americans had replaced earlier Native Americans through warfare. With this new evidence, they stepped up the fight to reclaim nonaffiliated skeletal remains and repatriation and reburial laws started to become more lenient in their requirements for affiliation.

Another controversial topic that has been studied is that of interpersonal aggression or violence in prehistory. In the 1960s, a backlash occurred against the depiction of prehistoric populations as violent savages; past populations, from Neanderthals to American Indians were portrayed in the 60s as living in peace with harmony to nature as well. This carefully constructed image was soon to be destroyed by the evidence emerging out of the ground. Large skeletal samples made available through salvage sites began to be studied for evidence of violence. What anthropologists discovered was that prehistoric populations on the North American continent had slews of injuries that could have only arisen through aggressive acts towards one another. For example, broken noses were common in a nearly all populations studied. Arrowheads lodged in human remains were also present; even Kennewick Man had such an injury. In the population housed as San Jose State University, we have nearly half a dozen individuals with arrowheads in their bones, from their backs to their chins (Figures 1 and 2). In some populations, scarce food and land resources are an easy explanation for these aggressive acts, such as in Eskimos. They certainly had lots of reasons to fight and their levels of violence were not seen again until the Industrial Age. In the Chilean desert, anthropologists have found high levels of violence that escalated with expanding chieftainship. This could have been due to political conflicts coupled with the fight for resources. There are others reasons to fight or not to fight that go beyond these specific examples.

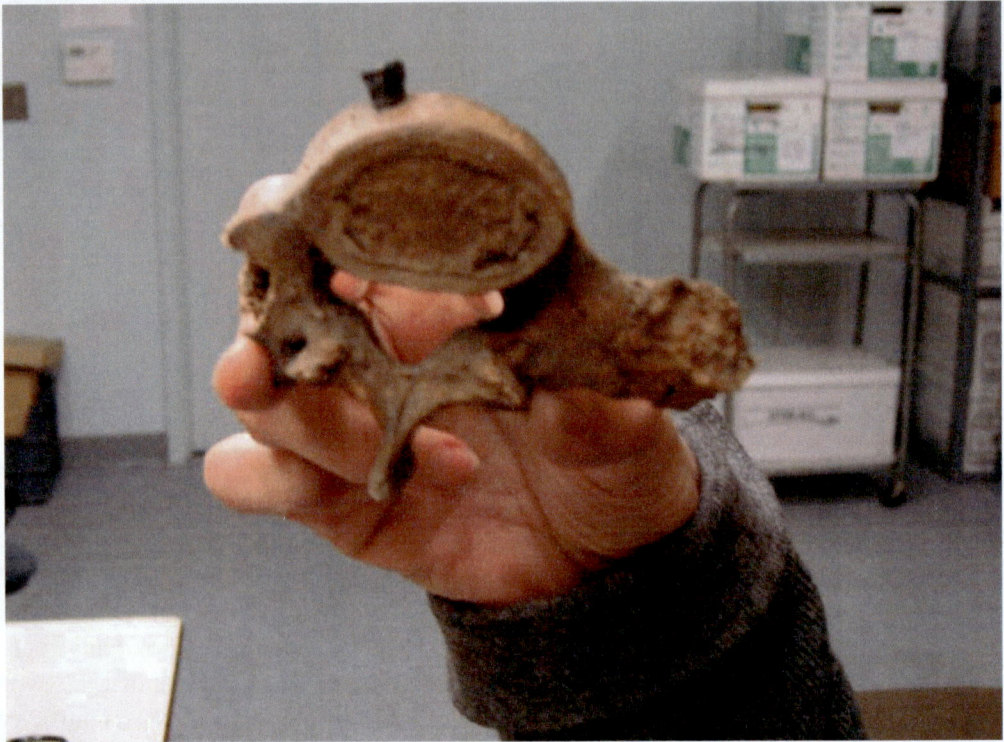

Figure 1. These are photographs of two different lumbar vertebrae (or lower back bone) with obsidian flakes in them, which were probably tips of arrowheads. The one individual likely lived through this injury since the obsidian is covered in bone and it appears that the bone grew over the obsidian. The other individual was not so lucky. These remains are from the CA-ALA-329 population housed at San Jose State University dated between 500 AD to 1500 AD (which is pre-European contact).

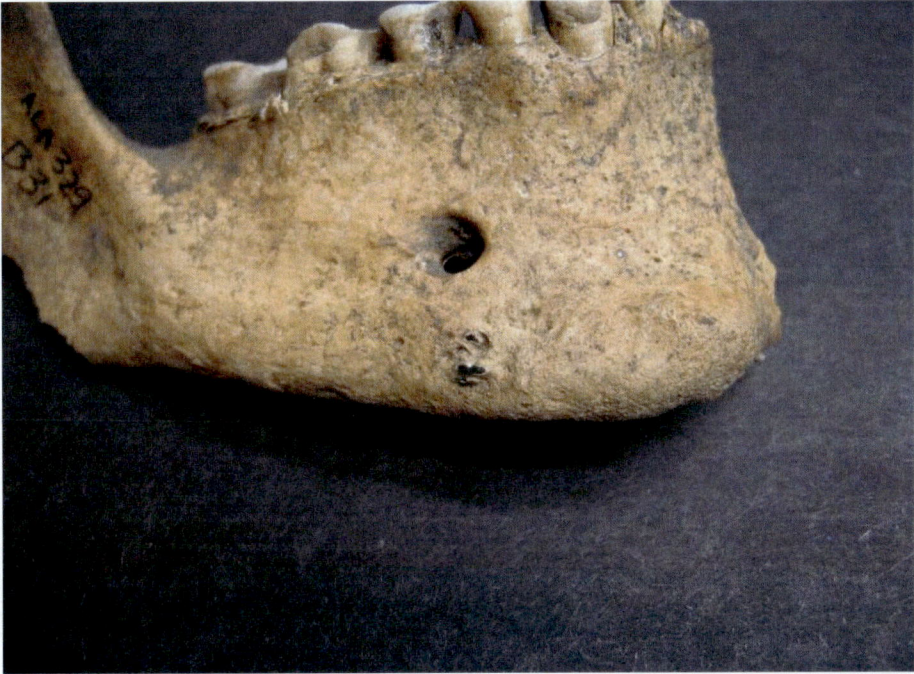

Figure 2. This is a photo of an adult male's lower jaw from the CA-ALA-329 hunter-gatherer population. In this individual's jaw, we see obsidian flakes from an arrowhead.

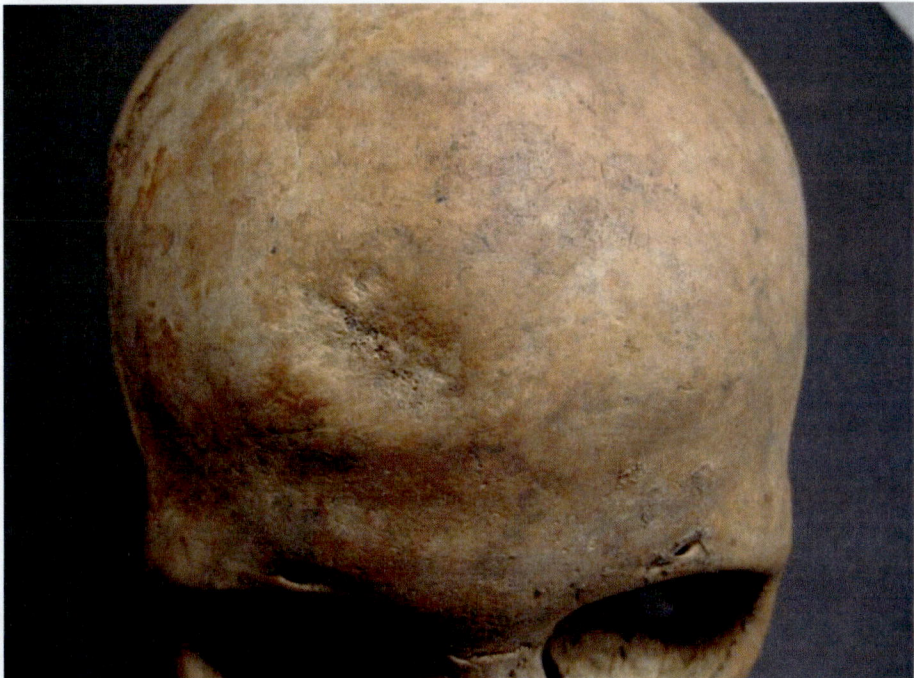

Figure 3. This photograph is taken from a 30-something year-old male from San Jose State University's collection; this individual has a large dent in the forehead that is the result of interpersonal violence. It is not likely to have caused the individual's death since the injury looks healed, but there are others who have no signs or few signs of healing.

Anthropologists, including in my own studies, have found consistent patterns of violence regardless of time and place. I conducted a small study on the California hunter-gatherer population housed at San Jose State University that looked at indications of violence on the skull and face; these parts of the body are the most often used because they are less likely to be injured through accidents. Arms, for example, can be broken in a number of ways, but how you get a big dent in the forehead is usually by being hit (Figure 3). In the hunter-gatherer peoples I was looking at six percent of individuals had injuries that were consistent with being a victim of violence; now remember we are just looking at skeletal remains and, therefore, more injuries probably occurred. So, at least 1 out of 16 individuals were hurt in the head by another individual. Now, we don't know if this was in-group violence, such as fights in the community and tribe, or warfare that may have involved other tribes.

A pattern emerged from my study that is common in other populations. Males are more often injured than females and when females are injured it is on the back of the head. This tells anthropologists that women were more likely victims and hit from behind whereas in males face-to-face combat was likely; we see this in the Californians I studied, throughout the Southwest, up in the Northern areas of British Columbia, and in many other places. Sex differences are often biological in nature and testosterone has been implicated in aggressive behavior, which could be why males are engaging in face-to-face combat and are presently more aggressive from bar fights to war. Research by psychologists Ralf Lindman from Finland and his colleagues Anu Aromäki, and CJ Peter Eriksson have linked testosterone to aggressive and antisocial behavior cross-culturally. Higher male facial trauma could be related to an evolutionary adaptation. Females were most likely selected to avoid risk and aggression, which could put them and their offspring in jeopardy. Sexual selection could also increase male aggression if females are choosing aggressive males who would fight for access to resources. Exceptions have been found and some these exceptions can be explained through maternal protection of young; for example, anthropologist Nancy Lovell has found female gorillas to be particularly aggressive when they have offspring that need protection.

Another pattern in nearly all cultures comes with age, children are not often found with injuries of the head, which would suggest that all cultures protect their kids from getting involved in violent activities. From an evolutionary perspective, it would be disastrous for the youngest individuals to become injured and perhaps die before they have a chance to reproduce. So, selection for protection of young, such as maternal care, may be one reason that we do not see as many facial injuries in subadults than in adults.

A further interesting fact has arisen through the study of skeletal remains in regards to violence and that is we do not find evidence of child abuse. We cannot prove that child abuse did not occur, but we can say that when examining skeletons of children in prehistory we have yet to find any patterns of injuries that are similar to those found in child abuse cases in forensic studies. Could it be that prehistoric populations were aware that their children were their future and, thus, didn't engage in the brutality that occurs in our modern day populations?

The bottom line on violence in prehistory is that we may want to hold on to the image of the Noble Savage (and there are some bright areas with low levels of violence and we don't see children victims often) and argue that violence is a relatively recent development, but the skeletons have painted a truer picture. The truth is that violence has always occurred and that regardless of whether you have farmers, hunter-gatherers, or modern populations, people can be aggressive. This aggression can increase when fighting for resources, such as food or oil. On the other hand, overall patterns are best explained through evolution.

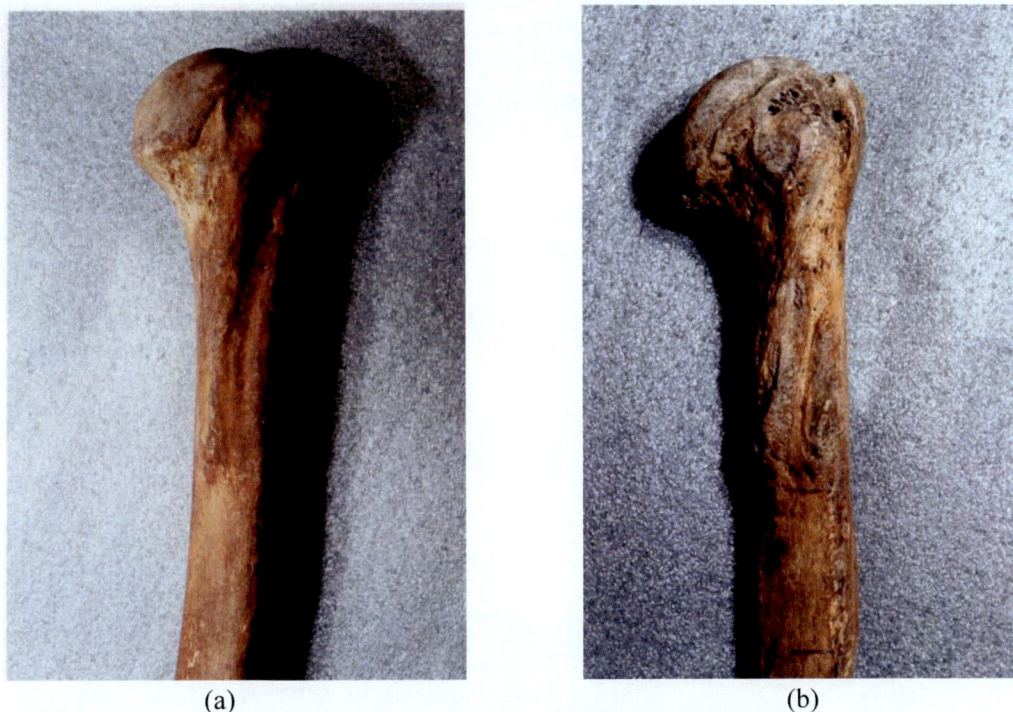

(a)   (b)

Figures 4. The above two photos are of humeri (upper arm bones) from British Columbian prehistoric hunter-gatherer population. (a) On the left side, we see a humerus that is a good example small muscle markings; (b) while the right humeri has large muscle markers. These photos were taken by Jerry Cybulski, courtesy of the Canadian Museum of Civilization.

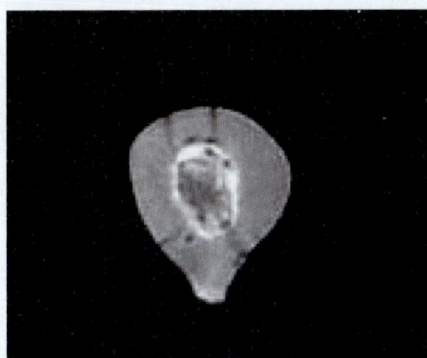

Figure 5. This is a CT-scan of Kennewick Man's CT-scanned mid-thigh bone. The large extension of the bone towards the bottom is indicative of his extensive walking and perhaps on treacherous terrains. Considering Kennewick Man's age of around 40 years of age, he also had very thick and, therefore, healthy bones. It is very likely, he died from an injury to the hip and he has an arrowhead in his hip joint.

Not all of bioarchaeology research involves controversial issues, such as those mentioned above. Hundreds of anthropologists use human remains to answer questions involved in reconstructing the everyday lives of past peoples. Some popular issues surround sex differences in activity, shifts in health related to the environment or agriculture, and aging patterns. Much of my own research revolves around the examination of muscle markers (which are locations on the bones where muscles attach and the more a muscle is used the rougher these areas are, in theory at least) (Figures 4a, b), cross-sectional studies using CT-scans (Figure 5) and X-rays (Figure 6) to see bone strength, and osteoarthritis patterns. All of these traits are used to reconstruct activity patterns; in other words, I am interested in knowing who was doing what in various cultures. Most of my research has been in the realm of fine-tuning the collection of data to cancel out the "noise" of body size and age. Rather recently, I have been able to control for some of the noise of body size to determine in the California population housed at San Jose State University, which had a division of labor even though they did not have agriculture. This hunter-gatherer population had signs of males doing the hunting, as in spear throwing for example, whereas female muscle markers were not as developed for these types of activities. Most likely females were grinding acorns and gathering other vegetation. Part of why this is interesting is because some anthropologists have argued that division of labor is a by-product of progress and that early hunter-gatherers were not divided in their labor (or at least less so than agriculturalists), but there is a bigger picture to be considered.

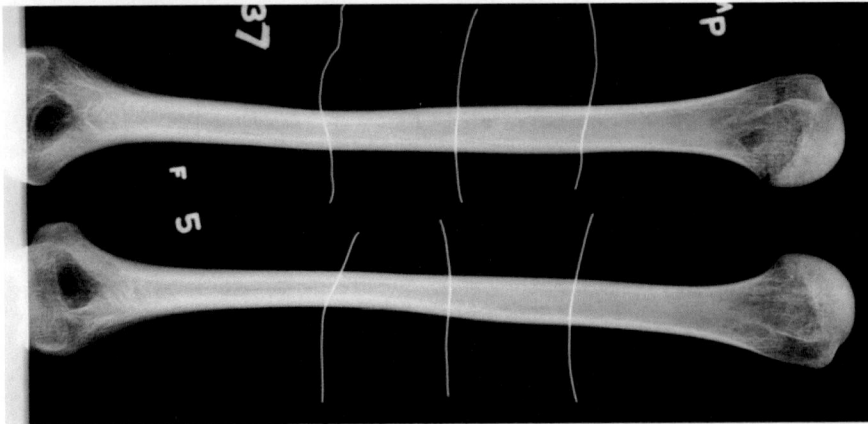

Figure 6. This X-ray is an example of data that I took for my doctoral dissertation in order to calculate bone strength and try to reconstruct activity patterns.

This data on preagricultural Amerindians goes beyond our understanding of one population and even stretches into how we understand ourselves. I remember sitting at a keynote lecture in the Human Behavior and Evolution Society Conference where the speaker was going on about how prehistoric diets of Native Americans were varied and lacked a staple starch and, therefore, we should follow their pattern in order to become healthy again. The keynote speaker, an evolutionary psychologist (which is a type of psychologist who tries to understand modern behavior through the lens of evolution) with no history of osteological research, failed to learn some very key things about past peoples revealed by bioarchaeologists only in the last decade. One thing is that we now know that in places where resources were rich, such as in California, people lived much more like farmers than in edge community hunter-gatherers. How this manifests itself is that hunter-gatherers would use a staple starch whenever it was available; California hunter-gatherers, for instance, consumed a great deal of acorns. So, instead of grinding maize as in the Southwest agricultural populations, California females were grinding acorns. This stable source of calories meant they were able to have high population densities in California as in agricultural areas since they also had a stable food source. Correspondingly, health indicators of hunter-gatherer Californians are more similar to early farmers than to other hunter-gatherers; for example, many of the individuals died of infection. Infection is only commonly spread when you get crowded situations and this is only commonly seen after the adoption of agriculture in most areas, but California was different. So, early Amerindians did have a staple starch in their diet, which allowed them to grow their population sizes.

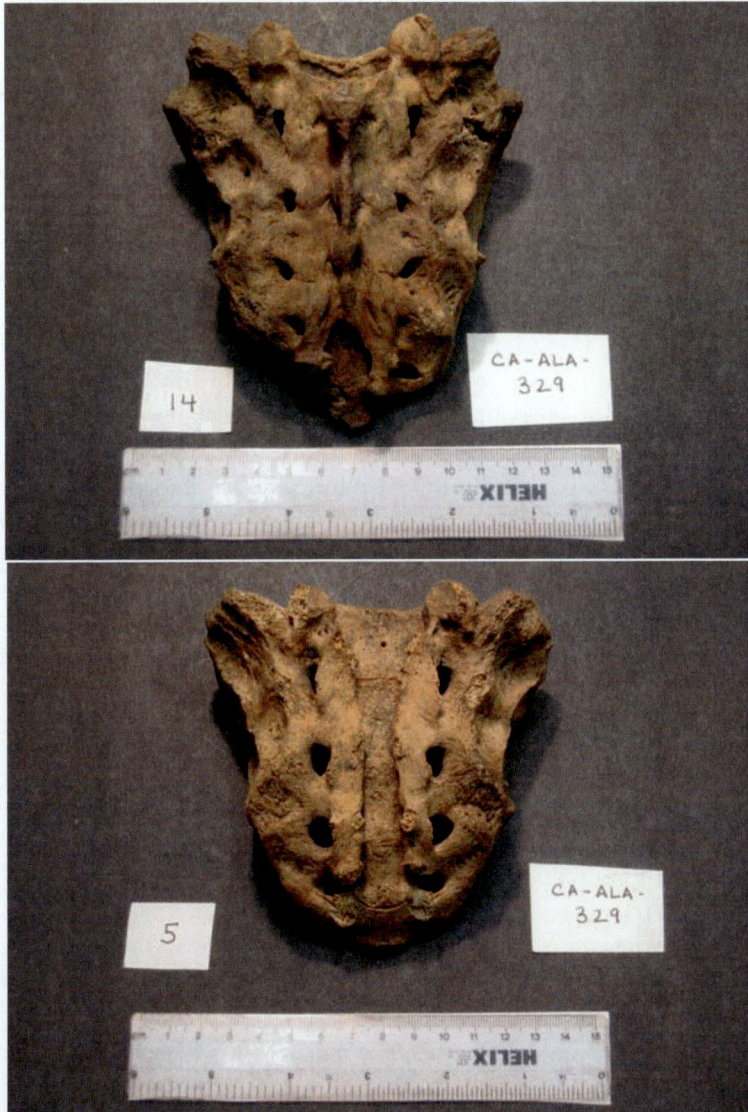

Figures 7. These two photos show sacra (which are the bones at the end of the vertebral column or back bone) of prehistoric Amerinds housed at San Jose State University. (a) On top is the sacrum of an adult who was born with a normally fused sacrum; (b) on bottom is the sacrum of an adult that was born with spina bifida occulta.

Additionally, the average age of death was only around 32 years old, which meant that they didn't suffer from osteoarthritis, but could hardly be held up as a good example for the way to stay healthy. Other indicators of low health are seen in congenital disorders. The incidence of spina bifida occulta was extremely high in Native Californians. Spina bifida occulta (Figures 7a, b) is a minor congenital disorder, but it is important as an indicator of the more severe spina bifida cases that are rarely seen in the bioarchaeological record because they usually cause death of the newborns. Spina bifida is when the backbones fail to fuse and leave the spinal cord exposed, which can lead to paralysis, retardation, and at worst even anacephaly (lack of a head or true brain). Modern medicine can intervene with in utero surgery to minimize the effects of spina bifida, but prior to these surgeries spina bifida often meant death at birth or shortly afterwards. Spina bifida has been greatly reduced in the last 50 years because of the fortification of folates in foods, such as cereals. Unfortunately, we are seeing a new increase in spina bifida with the consumption of low quality fast foods and unexpected births (there has been World Health Organization recommendations that all women of child bearing age take prenatal vitamins to prevent spina bifida in case of an unplanned pregnancy).

Interestingly, bioarchaeological research has found that ancient Egyptians had hardly any spina bifida occulta in their populations, which is most likely the result of their high lentil consumption. Lentils are a food high in folate and are still a large part of the Egyptian diet; Egyptian cases of spina bifida are lower than elsewhere in the Third World. As a result, although the Egyptians were agriculturalists and the Californians were hunter-gatherers; the Egyptians actually were eating healthier than the Californians! Without studying human remains, we could never have learned all these interesting variations in prehistory and would have assumed that hunter-gatherers were all similar (most like hunter-gatherers from the ethnographic records) and that agriculturalists were all similar. We also should avoid romanticizing the health of the past and instead look to what the real health indicators have revealed.

We have learned a great deal about shifts in culture through the study of human remains. One of the most important changes that occurred in prehistory was the onset of agriculture. Since this adoption of a new way of life occurred prior to written records, the only information we can obtain is through artifacts and skeletal remains. What we have learned is shocking. Agriculture has allowed for the development of large populations and eventually city states. Agriculture also decreased things like tooth wear, but we see our first major onset of cavities with agriculture, individuals become slightly shorter where agriculture is adopted, and infections of all sorts increase dramatically. These ill health indicators are the result of the increase in population density that is enabled through a steady food source. As mentioned previously, some places, such as California, didn't need agriculture to grow their populations and we see a large number of infections on these individuals as well.

One might think that in prehistory death would be most likely be due to injuries, but people cared for their injured group members as early as 1.8 million years ago and this continues throughout prehistory. Infection is the number one killer in prehistory and dental disease is often the source of that infection (Figure 8). Sometimes the dental problems arise due to cavities, such as when maize was the staple food, but it can also be due to congenital dental problems from inbreeding. With the onset of agriculture, people are moving around a lot less and they are mating with individuals more often related to them. This causes

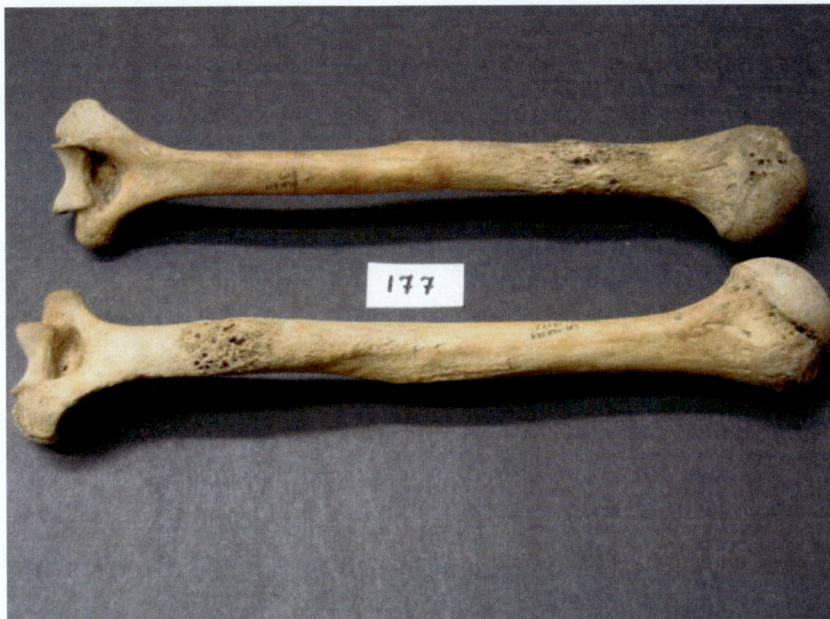

Figure 8. These arm bones come from an adult in the CA-ALA-329 population and display infection called periostitis, which is an infection that has spread throughout the body and has cloacae that are openings in the bones (and suggest openings to the skin while the person was living) where pus would have oozed out of the infected areas.

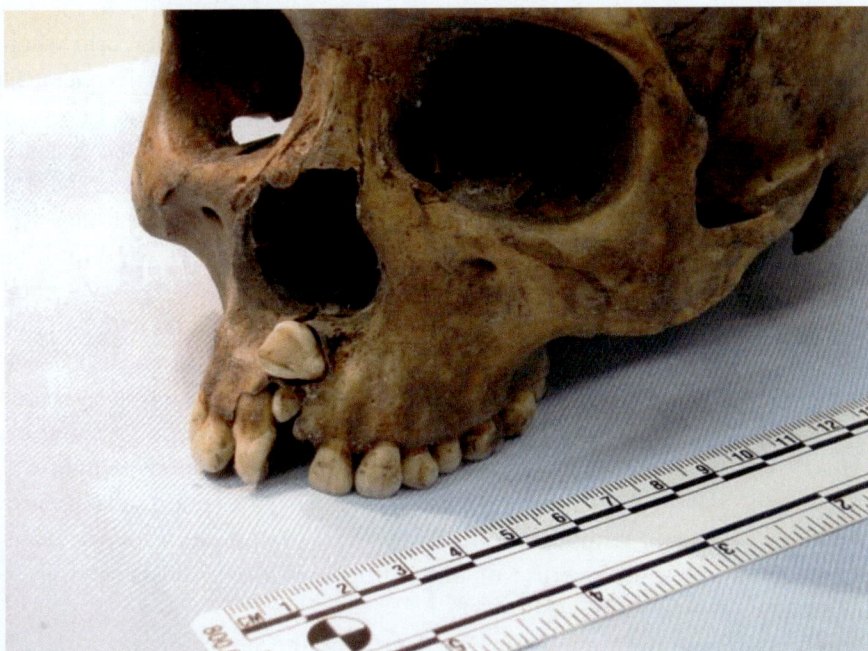

Figure 9. Burial 92 from CA-ALA-329 is from a young female who had a number of congenital issues. She had supernumerary teeth (one of which is coming out of her upper jaw bone right underneath her nose), she also had a cleft palate, and her whole bone appears to have been infected likely due to the dental abnormalities. She could have easily died from these problems.

extra teeth (known as supernumeraries) and teeth coming out in awkward ways (Figure 9); in modern days, a dentist could fix these problems prior to the child being harmed by the anomaly. However, in times prior to dental medicine these things could be deadly. Consequently, agriculture allowed for a population growth, but not a healthier group of people since nutrition decreased, inbreeding increased, and infections ran rampant.

Other infectious diseases have been of great interest to anthropologists. Syphilis has been a point of discussion for decades. Syphilis comes in three forms; two are not venereal while the third is a venereal disease (also known as a sexually transmitted disease). All three forms are bacterial and cannot be easily distinguished from one another in lab tests. Basically, where one sees venereal syphilis, one doesn't commonly see the other types. Syphilis creates saber-shaped shins, loss of bone, especially in the nasal and palatine areas (which is the roof of the mouth), and destruction of the skull. Venereal syphilis is more severe than the other forms in that it not only attacks the bone and cartilage, but also the organs inside causing damage to the brain and the central nervous system. Syphilis is treatable through antibiotics. Anthropologists have long been concerned with the spread of syphilis and using skeletal samples they have tried to ascertain whether syphilis was in the Old World (which consists of Europe, Asia, and Africa) prior to the return of Columbus or whether Columbus brought back syphilis from his journeys to the Americas. There is some evidence from skeletal material that suggest syphilis originated in the New World (which consists of the North, Central, and South America). In research published in 2000, anthropologist Dr. Bruce Rothschild and his colleagues found no evidence of syphilis in Europe, Africa, Asia, or the Middle East prior to the return of Columbus in 1490s. Yet, there was an endemic syphilis outbreak throughout Europe in 1500. He also found the earliest cases of non-venereal syphilis in the New World around 1600 years ago (or 400 AD). His suggestion is that in the New World where climate was warm, syphilis was non-venereal and spread easily through normal contact (such as a common cold nowadays), but that when this bacteria was taken overseas to Europe it evolved quickly. Clothed individuals in Europe made the bacteria hard to be passed on and presumably some mutation allowed some bacteria to be passed through sex; these were then the best adapted bacteria and the disease spread throughout Europe. Besides the skeletal evidence, we see in modern societies where venereal syphilis occurs we do not have other forms of the bacteria and visa versa.

I frequently ask my classes what the number one killer in the world is today; they usually guess AIDS or cancer, but the correct answer is tuberculosis. Tuberculosis (also known as TB) is a bacterial infection that attacks the lungs; it also destroys bone tissue and can be seen in the vertebral column, which then causes the back bones to collapse crushing organs and breaking ribs. Symptoms of individuals living with TB include a bloody cough, weight loss, night sweats, and painful breathing. It can also affect the brain and destroy joints. Tuberculosis can be cured with antibiotics, but new strains are evolving resistance to antibiotics, especially with the overuse of these drugs and the inconsistent follow through when people are prescribed antibiotics.

Anthropologists have been attempting to determine the origin of this killer (in part to understand its path and to perhaps halt its further spread). Previously, most of us have been taught that TB was brought to the Americas by Columbus and this in fact killed many Native Americans. Conversely, anthropologists are reexamining this theory to determine whether it holds up under more scrutiny. Egyptian mummies have signs of TB as far back as 5000 years ago. This seems to support the Old World origin. In the 2003 book *The Bioarchaeology of*

Tuberculosis professors Charlotte Roberts of the University of Durham in England and Jane Buikstra of Arizona State University outline some evidence that may suggest an additional origin of TB. There has arisen some new evidence from DNA that is pre-contact in Peruvian and Chilean mummies. These studies are fairly recent and we have yet to find conclusive evidence in skeletons of North America to support a New World origin for tuberculosis. With skeletons being buried, unfortunately, the evidence may also be buried.

Figure 10. This is the backbone of an adult male with spondylolysis. He would have perhaps felt pain associated with this fracture, but in life the two separated pieces would have been held together by muscles and tissue.

Common problems for prehistoric populations include spinal stress fractures. One of my favorite quotes is from Dr. Don Johanson the famous anthropologist who found the 3.6 million year-old skeleton Lucy. He said: "As remarkable as our adaptations for bipedalism are, they are, like all evolutionary transformations, a compromise with history." This is incredibly true since evolution does not start anew for new species, but rather just makes moderate changes on old designs. Our back problems are a legacy of our quadrupedal (walking on hands and feet) past. One thing that we get due to this evolutionary past is stress fractures called spondylolysis. This is when a back bone separates the front and back (Figure 10); in a living person this bone is held together by muscles and other tissues. But, in the skeletal collections, we see these as separate pieces of bone. Some populations have very few of these stress fractures (like British populations) whereas other populations have a great number of them with over 50% of the population having had a fracture. The Californian prehistoric peoples I studied had about 20% of the individuals affected, which is quite high. Dr. Charles Merbs, an anthropologist with an expertise on these fractures and a long history

Figures 11. Even though CA-ALA-329 individuals have low levels of osteoarthritis, here are two examples of osteoarthritis. (a) The top example comes from the lower back and this is most commonplace to have osteoarthritis. The cartilage between the backbones has deteriorated and bone rubbing on bone causes a reaction of bone to grow and mobility has been lost in this portion of the back, such as in the fused bones pictured here. (b) This second example is on the ulna of an adult; this would have hindered or made wrist movement painful.

of studying artic populations, noted certain trends regardless of culture. For example, our primate cousins never get these fractures, we only see these fractures occurring in people old enough to walk, and the lower back is most commonly afflicted. Coupling these patterns with the evidence from sports medicine that show unusually high numbers of these fractures in gymnasts; Merbs has successfully hypothesized that stress fractures in the lower back may actually be a way for humans to cope with being bipedal – walking on two legs. He suggests there is an advantage to getting these fractures and that advantage is flexibility. It appears that having fractures like these increases flexibility or, of course, it could be that flexible individuals stress out their backs. Regardless, it was the ability to research human remains that opened up the study of these fractures. It has enabled us another way of understanding how evolution works and the effect of evolution on our bodies and lives.

Osteoarthritis may have been the most prevalent disease in our biological prehistory, which makes sense since these individuals worked a great deal and osteoarthritis is usually explained as over use of joints with cartilage wearing away and results in growth of bony spicules that limit joint mobility (Figures 11a, b). Osteoarthritis is an age-related disease and, so, in some peoples like the population housed at San Jose State University where we have very few old individuals (with most of them dying of dental diseases and infections) there are correspondingly low levels of osteoarthritis. Osteoarthritis, therefore, can be thought of as a good indicator of population health because it goes hand in hand with old age. When we see osteoarthritis in younger individuals, on the other hand, we can use it to reconstruct activity patterns (or what people were doing). For example, certain joints that are used excessively due to activities may be prone to osteoarthritic changes earlier in life. The late Dr. Patricia Bridges, famous for her studies on women's work in prehistory, found significant osteoarthritis in female neck bones of Alabama prehistoric Indians. She associated this early onset of osteoarthritis with the fact that women may have been carrying objects on their heads; this is supported by later artifacts of carrying bags made to fit on the head and suggest a continuum of culture in this part of the Americas. Other areas of the Americas have seen a continuation of cultural practices that can be reconstructed using osteoarthritis frequency, such as the use of an atlatl (a type of spear thrown for hunting) by Aleuts and prehistoric Alaskan populations (documented in Dr. Merb's research). Old age diseases other than osteoarthritis are not commonly seen in prehistoric populations. For example, cancers are rare; broken hips are not common either. Heart disease also is difficult, if not impossible, to diagnose on a skeletal individual.

By looking at the skull and other parts of the body, we can understand cultural practices of past peoples. Biodistance studies conducted on Pueblo Indians in Arizona, New Mexico, Colorado, and Utah between 1350 and 1680 AD give us evidence of marital patterns (see Larsen, 2003). The skulls of males varied a good deal more than did the skulls of females, which suggests that the culture was matrilocal. A matrilocal culture is one in which females stay with their mother's group and males migrate out to join other groups. Thus, the problem of inbreeding is avoided by males moving into new groups. Other populations have patrilocal cultures where females move out (sometimes female are stolen from their home groups). Finally, we see low degrees of variation in skulls were there is a lot of in-group breeding, sometimes producing congenital anomalies (or birth defects, such as extra fingers and toes). Gene flow is also marked by dental traits, since like skulls, dentition is genetically fixed. We see that in the Carolinas, where resources were rich, there is not much variation and populations were steady. In Georgia and Florida the populations were quite different from the

Carolina populations, which can be inferred to suggest that these populations did not interbreed along the southeast coast. This may be related to the rich resources and the lack of requirement for peoples to trade and form collaborations in the Carolinas. In South America, anthropologists found sacrificial victims dated around 200 – 750 AD; they asked the question of who these victims were in Northern Peru. Through an examination of skulls and dentition they found the sacrificed individuals were significantly different from local skulls; they appeared to be nonlocal warriors who ended up as prisoners of war and eventually were sacrificed. Hence, dentition and skull anatomy tells more than just who was related to who, but marriage patterns, migration and trade routes, and sacrificial victim identities.

Another interesting effort for anthropologists is to understand juvenile ailments as an indicator of overall population health. Anthropologists have used Harris Lines (which are seen on X-rays of the shin bone, Figure 12) to determine the number of times growth has temporarily stopped for juvenile individuals. Growth may stop due to a lack of food, infections, or parasites. When growth stops and then starts again, then we see this as a horizontal line on shin bone X-rays. Previously, these lines have been related to ill health and thought of as a negative sign, but recently anthropologists have reassessed the meaning of Harris Lines (and their dental counterparts – enamel hypoplasia). Now, adult skeletons found with these health indicators are actually thought of as the individuals who were best off; they actually lived through episodes of stress and made it to adulthood. Thus, one can see how science is self-correcting, but also that sometimes information provides two types of information: that of childhood illness and that of recovering from illness.

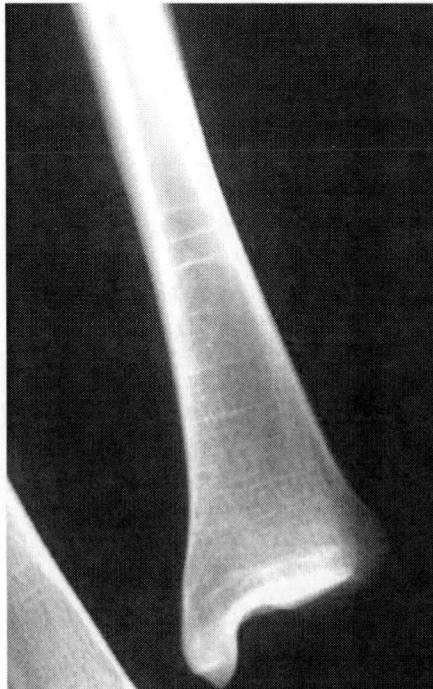

Figure 12. Harris lines displayed here are signs of growth disturbance due to a variety of possible factors, such as malnutrition, parasites, and infections. Some people consider these lines as indicators of being healthy enough to recover from these hardships and that the absence of Harris lines does not necessarily mean the individuals were better off (especially if we are looking at only juvenile remains).

In summary, studying skeletal remains provides us with a vast number of answers to many important questions. Anthropologist Philip Walker, who was a past president of the American Association of Physical Anthropologists, wrote in the 2006 book *Biological Anthropology and Ethics* that the information gained through studying skeletal remains tells us about our adaptability, our evolution, our prehistoric changes, and relates to us today. He further adds that the information hidden in the bones is immutable, unlike the oral traditions that are passed on. Truth lies within the bones. If we want to know who the Indians of prehistoric America were, then we need to obtain the answers through the study of human remains, not through oral traditions.

USING HUMAN REMAINS TO ANSWER RESEARCH QUESTIONS: NEW QUESTIONS INVOLVE RESTUDYING COLLECTIONS THAT HAVE ALREADY BEEN STUDIED

One of the hardest things to get students and other people to understand is that there is little need for new skeletal collections for most research. My students often desire entirely unstudied collections to conduct their research and I emphasize to them that this is actually disadvantageous, especially for a Master's degree (which is a two-year post baccalaureate degree). Why would one want to study the same samples over and over again? It is because the interest is not in the specific skeletal collection being examined, but rather in the question being asked.

Science works through asking new questions and re-testing old answers. It is a method of re-examining what has been done using the same techniques, different techniques, and different samples. Only through replication can we come up with natural laws. Evolution has not been proven through one study. Just like the examination of violence in prehistory had to be studied and studied again with different samples and in different methods to really understand human prehistory and human nature. When we replicate previously produced results, then we can start to say with more certainty that these results are telling us the true picture of the past. So, we use our sample at San Jose State University to answer questions that have been previously answered using other samples. This helps to determine whether things are culturally specific or universal. If something is repeatedly found, like men get hit in the front of their face more often than women, then we can say that this is human nature rather than culture. We can say this only if we have looked at populations from all over the world and from various times.

When we see these universals, such as men having larger muscle markers than women, we must then determine what caused this. Muscle markers are used to reconstruct what people did in the past. As mentioned earlier, these are raised locations on bones where muscles attach and when the muscles are used these locations get rougher. By looking at just one population, you may conclude that the men were more active than the women, but then if you know that this muscle marker pattern is found nearly everywhere another cause may be present. I have replicated the sex difference in muscle markers in many populations and I have found that the cause seems in part to be size; larger people have larger muscle markers. And, thus, people who just look at one sample may be underestimating the work women were doing! Knowing these confounds, knowing what the true causes are can help us dissect the traits used to reconstruct the past and draw a more accurate picture. For example, if you control for body size, you can see that both females and males were extremely active in the California hunter-gatherer population that I looked at, but males used their arms more for hunting and throwing spears, while females gathered.

What becomes very interesting is when you get a reversal in the pattern; these reversals highlight culturally specific activities. In back stress fractures, we know that males are more often to get them than females, but there are exceptions to the higher male spondylolysis frequency trend. One exception with well-documented ethnohistorical evidence comes from studies published by Dr. Karl Reinhard and his colleagues in the mid-1990s on the northeastern Nebraska Amerinds; females were responsible for hide scraping, house construction, and gathering firewood. In these Nebraskans, females had greater spondylolysis frequencies than their male counterparts. Consequently, only through studying the same question in many ways and in many populations can we understand what is related to biology and what is related to activity. It is so important to be able to re-ask the same question.

On the flip side, there are new questions to be asked using previously studied samples. If a sample has already been studied, it does not mean that it is ready for reburial because it has no more value. Skeletal samples can be used over and over again for new questions. For instance, we may ask more questions concerning osteoarthritis, such as how can we best understand osteoarthritis in young individuals in prehistory. Other questions that may arise concern growth patterns, the cause of death, how to use traits to reconstruct activities, and many more. When you ask new questions using previously studied samples, you reduce time to conduct the research since things like sex, age, and time period will already be covered. This allows for a fast moving field of science that gives us more and more answers to the past.

So, one can see that science is not just about having a new sample and then describing the sample, but rather it is about asking questions and answering these questions. When we get rid of skeletal samples, we lose the ability to answer more questions. We shouldn't be bound to just do descriptive studies on the human remains; this would be putting the field back over forty years when the theory of bioarchaeology had yet to be developed and articles were mere descriptions of skeletal material.

NEW TECHNIQUES THAT ALLOW FOR MORE ACCURATE RECONSTRUCTIONS

When human remains are reburied, we cannot re-examine questions using better techniques. In the 1980's, for example, DNA studies were practically unheard of in anthropology. Now, anthropologists have used DNA to determine the split of chimps and humans as well as between Neanderthals and *Homo sapiens*. The Neanderthal studies have been replicated and have shown that our last common ancestor with Neanderthal's was 600,000 years ago, suggesting that we never interbred with them and that they are a separate species. DNA studies on Paleo-Indians have not been as fruitful, but they are improving. Someday, if the bones are still available, we may be able to have a really accurate reconstruction of the peopling of the Americas.

DNA studies can also help us determine where diseases originated, such as syphilis and tuberculosis. It was once thought that tuberculosis was brought to the Americas by Columbus and killed off many Native Americans because they had no immunity to it. Ancient DNA of tuberculosis found in a South American mummy, however, predates Columbus meaning that there is evidence of TB prior to the European invasion of the New World. We don't know how it got to North America perhaps tuberculosis has two origins. These disease studies are just starting to take shape and without the human remains, we cannot answer questions concerning the diseases.

Other new technology emerging is three-dimensional scanning and laser technology. These imaging tools will help us better understand the morphology of the Native Americans. Kennewick Man was first reconstructed as looking like Patrick Steward the actor from Star Trek, but more recent reconstructions have him looking more Native American. The true face of Kennewick Man will only come about with more research and that research will likely require new technologies.

My own research, as I mentioned earlier, has been involved in determining what controls need to be done in order to better reconstruct the past. We have already seen that muscle markers, those points on bones were muscles insert and are used to reconstruct activity, differ between the sexes and often males have larger muscle markers, but this is confounded with the problem of body size. We don't want to mistakenly assert that males were working harder when it is just that their bodies are bigger and, as a result, they have larger muscle markers. The opposite is true for osteoarthritis; in modern populations heavier people have more osteoarthritis (especially of weight bearing joints), but in prehistory smaller jointed (and most presumably smaller people) had more osteoarthritis. This difference is slight, but likely due to the fact that the smaller joint has less surface area to distribute the force on it. When looking at modern humans, the most affected individuals actually are the ones with heavy bodies and small joints (females). What this means is that we can understand the present through the past and use the entire body of knowledge to reconstruct the past more accurately as well and try to change the present patterns. We must be careful of reconstructing activities without taking biology into account. In addition, new studies of old materials may be conducted to reexamine reconstructions using osteoarthritis and muscle markers with these new controls; this could result in providing us with a clearer picture of what people were doing and prevent the over emphasis on male activities as we have seen in the past.

What do we still have to figure out? Isn't 50 years of answering questions about the past enough? Well, anthropologists are still trying to determine how syphilis and tuberculosis spread. We are still trying to determine ways to reconstruct specific activities, especially those that may not have been done routinely. Past populations are still a mystery in many ways.

Chapter 3

ANTHROPOLOGISTS AS THE GOOD GUYS

"The professionals of today cannot be classed with the plunderers of the past, and frequently the disturbance of burials is purely accidental."

Kevin Sharpe and Helen Fawbert (2007: Whose Heritage?
The Conflict between Living and the Dead within Archaeology.
Science and Spirit Magazine).

HOW ANTHROPOLOGISTS HAVE OBTAINED SKELETAL COLLECTIONS: SALVAGE SITES AND NATIVE AMERICAN REMAINS

As early as 1907, anthropologist Ales Hrdlicka, who founded the *American Journal of Physical Anthropology* and the American Association of Physical Anthropologists, was studying remains to reconstruct the prehistory of the Americas. His early studies were done on human remains from Louisiana, California, Mississippi, Florida, Colorado, South Carolina, Illinois, New Mexico, Kansas, New Jersey, Nebraska, and Canada. The remains were obtained in many ways some of which included deliberate excavation. On the other hand, much of the data was discovered inadvertently during the construction of buildings and the excavation of mines, which Kathleen Fine-Dare admits to in her 2002 book *Grave Injustice*.

Cressida Fforde, in her 2004 book *Collecting the Dead: Archaeology and the Reburial Issue*, notes that the collection of Native American and other remains created some of our greatest collections in the 19th Century; however, those days are over as I will explain in the following pages. Collection of remains in the United States, which consisted nearly entirely of Native American remains, was extremely competitive with scientists trying to beat out their colleagues by the number of bones in their collections. Douglas Cole in his 1985 book *Captured Heritage* examines the collection of Native American bones in the early days of American physical anthropology. Cole points out the legendary competition between Dr. Franz Boas who was the curator at the American Museum of Natural History in New York and Dr. George A. Dorsey, the past curator in Chicago's Field Museum. They both tried consistently to build the world's best anthropological museum; a noble goal, even if the methods were questionable for today' populace. Dr. Ales Hrdlicka was at the Smithsonian when he too jumped into the competitive realm of building skeletal collections and he created the world's best collection. His research was neither on intelligence nor race; rather, Dr. Hrdlicka examined the origins of Native Americans and tried to understand their prehistory. Thus, although much has been made of the excesses of the collecting and the aims of earlier studies, anthropologists were just trying to understand the world around them. Moreover, Dr. Boas studying skulls came to very politically palatable conclusions, that race wasn't fixed, there was a great deal of variation within each group, and no group had dominance on intelligence.

The situation has changed to one of infrequent deliberate excavations and most often salvage sites (which are sites where artifacts and human remains are found during construction or in other unintentional ways); the remains are then saved from just being destroyed. When people first hear about my profession as an anthropologist, they inquire about my fieldwork. I often get asked whether I plan to go on a dig during my summer break or when I am going to dig up some stuff in the future. I explain to them that this is not what I do. I am a lab anthropologist who conducts continuous research on remains that have already been uncovered. I try to emphasize to casual listeners and students that the important aspect of science is not the discovery of new materials, but the questions that are posed and eventually answered using previously discovered remains. When these individuals are friendly, I sense a disappointment on their faces, but sometimes this misperception can take on an unfriendly nature.

My own studies have been mainly conducted on human remains that have been uncovered decades ago when the California highway system was being built. My Master's thesis is on a collection that was salvaged from the San Joaquin valley while interstate highway five was being built. The remains are housed at Sacramento State University; this sample contained around 161 individuals who were uncovered in the 1960s and 70s. In the decades they were housed at the university, countless studies have been conducted on the remains. One of which was my own thesis that examined the activity differences between men and women in preagricultural California. The population housed at San Jose State University is also a salvage site, but one from Alameda (which is near the Bay Area). The site was discovered when highways were being expanded and the remains along with artifacts were removed and stored at the university. This collection has been extensively studied and yields new information each year on the past lives of people in California. In the short time I have been a professor here, I have conducted research on violence, spina bifida, arthritis, and activity patterns. My first graduate student conducted research on this population to determine the health of the juveniles in this population and whether their health changed with changes in the environment. A rich skeletal collection is a resource for scientists and the community (both Native Americans and others) who deserve to learn about the past. Although I have a strong history of research, this does not include my participation in removal of human remains. I do not desire to dig up any remains, but rather have a strong yen for learning what we can from those salvaged remains already in our presence.

MISPERCEPTIONS OF SCIENTISTS IN THE NATIVE AMERICAN COMMUNITY AND GENERAL PUBLIC

In 2006, I presented data on skeletal collections at the American Association for the Advancement of Science; this is the largest scientific organization in the world and each year they have a conference. Due to the importance of the conference, I decided to have a press release on my findings. The study, which was on the negative effects of NAGPRA on bioarchaeological research and will be discussed later in more detail, drew attention from many sides and I received many hostile e-mails following the event. Some of these e-mailers have the same misperception as my friendly inquirers that I go out and dig up human remains to then describe and study. For example, I received an e-mail from the Manataka American Indian Council entitled "Who's Digging Up Grandma's Bones?" that carried out this misperception with the line "So, you want to dig up my grandmother's bones for the benefit of your so-called scientific studies?" along with other misperceptions that I will return to. Another e-mail echoes a similar sentiment:

> "The Native American Graves Protection and Repatriation Act saves our Ancestors from being dug up and parked in a museum someplace. While the land they were laid to rest in is being used for a walmart parking lot .It is very disturbing to us to find out that people such as yourself has to recieve credibility on the remains of others .Do us a favor go and dig up your own Ancestors remains and please leave ours alone" [sic]

(from staff@nativeearthworkssociety.info)

This individual is in part correct; human remains have been removed from the earth in order to make room for construction, such as Wal-Mart, housing, interstates, and many more. The alternative to removing them would have been to destroy the remains. Anthropologists have been in the forefront of saving hundreds of thousands of skeletal remains from being destroyed by bulldozers, paving machines, demolition balls, and other tools of construction. Where this e-mailer is not correct is that anthropologists do study other populations. In Europe, human remains have also been salvaged and studied. If I were in Europe, I am sure those are the individuals I would be conducting my research on. European remains are not in as much of a threat of reburial due to a different culture; a culture of pride in human remains and what one can learn from them. When Otzi the 5,000 year-old iceman was discovered, Europeans didn't call for a funeral; instead they argued over whether the remains could be claimed as Italian or Austrian. The media and populace encouraged scientific inquiry into the cause of death, the origins, and the life of this past European. They erected billboards to advertise the importance of this find and even put Otzi on display with pride.

In a review of the repatriation literature, none of the individuals in favor of repatriation and reburial has brought up the fact that anthropologists do work on Caucasians as well. Caucasoid skeletons throughout the world have been the subjects of many studies; some of my own research has included non-Native American samples. Probably about 30% of bioarchaeological research is actually on Caucasian remains! A smattering of African, African-American, and Asian research continues to flourish as well.

As for the progress in the United States, construction has been inevitable. I am not in favor of the destruction of the American landscape through big box stores and cloned housing communities. Interstates and highways also do not warm my heart and I personally live without a car and in as environmentally-friendly manner as possible. Still, when these constructions occur (which they have and will continue to do), then human remains will be discovered. The options that are available to anthropologists and Native Americans are that we either let the past be destroyed by this "progress" or save the remains and their artifacts by removing them, which is indeed a noble enterprise. Once removed, should they be placed back into the ground? Most Native Americans and many scientists would say yes. I argue that no they shouldn't be reburied. The reasons behind my point of view will be addressed in full detail later, but just as a foreshadow of what is to come let me say that reburying bones destroys them and the ability to understand the people who lived before us.

PAYING FOR SINS OF THE PAST RESEARCHERS: JUDGING THE PAST THROUGH MODERN MORALITY

I remember sitting in my history of evolutionary theory course with professor Adrienne Zihlman, at the extremely liberal University of California at Santa Cruz, where she warned us not to judge past scientists by our own moral code. Even though she made it abundantly clear that this type of judgment was completely unacceptable, students still had difficulty divorcing their own morals from the morals of the past. One student in particular was in tears when she found out some of Charles Darwin's (who is the father of evolutionary theory and wrote the ground breaking book *Origin of Species* published in 1859) views on sex differences. Charles Darwin, by the standards of his era, was neither sexist nor racist; however, by our own standards, he may seem so. In the 2006 book *Imperialism, Art, and Restitution*, the authors Dr. Michael Brown from Williams College and Margaret Bruchac from University of Massachusetts, Amherst wrote right from the start in the chapter on NAGRPA that we should be ashamed of our past.

> "The implementation of NAGPRA prompted anthropologists to examine their profession with a critical eye, to weigh the thoughtless and sometimes shameful behavior of anthropology's intellectual ancestors against more recent efforts to set matters right."

Yet, past anthropologists and other scientists have been facing this retroactive judgment since the 1960s. Studies of brain size, intelligence, and group differences are continuously criticized without any thought of temporal relativity. Furthermore, little credit is given to those scientists (anthropologists in particular) who have debunked many of the old theories on group differences; Dr. Philip Walker mentions this repeatedly in his own work. Dr. Kathleen Fine-Dare, as late as 2002, does a thorough job at showing how anthropologists used skeletal material to rank races. She, nevertheless, also mentions that Franz Boas, the 'father of American anthropology,' was a strong advocate for equality and fought against the misuses of science. In order to aid in the demonstration of equality, Boas engaged in much research that involved skeletal analyses of Native American remains. Boas and other anthropologists were at the forefront of destroying racial groupings and discrimination and aiding the Civil Rights Movement in the US. This too is often not remembered or glossed over. So, even though there were anthropologists who did controversial research and research that has not held up in the years (such Dr. Samuel Morton's phrenology studies, which involved telling the character of an individual by the shape of the skull and face), other research has withstood the test of time.

Even worse than judging past peoples through our own moral lenses is expecting today's scientists to pay for those perceived past indiscretions. Anthropologists have been paying for the sins of earlier scientists for decades. There are countless books on the study of race differences and how anthropologists have a long past of ranking people with the Europeans ending up at the top of the ladder. We have apologized and shown due respect for those who come from the victimized groups. Nonetheless, this group victimization needs a group to be vilified. We, thus, continue to pay for the sins of our forefathers. I asked earlier whether I should feel guilty for my German ancestry due to the Holocaust and victimized for my Jewish ancestry. I cannot be held responsible for what anthropologists have done with bones in the past. While it is true that sometimes they used destructive methods (which were at times the only methods available) and sometimes they displayed remains in ways that are less than appropriate in today's world, they also had a sincere interest in learning about the past.

Early studies were not at all about disrespect and many continue to serve a purpose today. Early studies on the femur of different ethnic groups still help forensic anthropologists identify crime victims. Other early studies have helped us to understand our differences are in part due to climatic differences and this has in turn given us an understanding of where people came from. Information gained from early studies has provided us with a foundation for our new more sophisticated studies. Most often early studies were not evil, but rather just descriptive and anthropologists lacked the skills, collections, and sometimes technology to better answer what people's lives were like in the past.

Finally, many individuals who are in support of repatriation have classified all anthropological research as racist. Attorney Jerry Springer recently pointed out that some Native Americans perceive modern anthropologists as having the same mindset of European colonialists and state that anthropological theories are just a way to cover up racism. In Kathleen Fine-Dare's 2002 book *Grave Injustice*, the contributors have no qualms about calling anthropology irrelevant and anthropologists racists. Native Americans have latched onto this idea too that modern anthropologists are racists. For example, Suzan Harjo, an activist with the Morning Star Foundation, clearly states that she thinks that the study of Indians remains comes down to racism. What is often ignored is that American Indian remains are not singled out; as I pointed out earlier the Ice Man from Europe has been and continues to be studied extensively, there are famous autopsy collections housed in New Mexico and Ohio, mummies of the Old and New World are continuously being examined too. Even DNA tests on historic figures are common, such as the last Tsar of Russia and President Zachary Taylor. Dr. Amy Dansie, at the Nevada State Museum, has been quoted in the *Nevada Journal* as saying: "If the Nevada State Museum is racist, it has an odd way of demonstrating its bigotry" since NAGPRA's passing remains have been repatriated expeditiously.

RESPECT FOR HUMAN REMAINS GAINED THROUGH KNOWLEDGE

Respect is a term that is too often thrown around without a comprehension of the true meaning of the word. We hear that you have to respect your elders and often times minority groups ask for respect from the government or from the majority group. I have had students ask for respect when they don't show the same towards their professors. Let me define respect before I continue. Respect refers to holding a high opinion on something or showing reverence to the thing or person. Respect, consequently, should not be automatic, but rather should be earned. I try to earn the respect of my peers through conducting high quality research. I try to earn the respect of my students by providing them with useful information through an interesting approach that I hope they will find relevant and enhance their comprehension of the world around them. I don't expect students to walk in to my class holding reverence towards me, but I expect them to come in with an open mind and I certainly hope to gain their respect.

How this relates to skeletal material is that I started to hold human remains in high regard once I started to understand what information they could provide us. Through reading about research on remains and starting to understand the lives people led prior to the industrial period, I began to value the remains and the people who study them. Thus, contrary to what many may think, I have a huge deal of respect for human remains. This respect has been earned, as all respect should be. How it manifests itself is that I treat the human remains well. I never consume foods or liquids around them since that may attract pests; I always put them back in their appropriate places, and I handle them with care. I don't make jokes using the bones of these individuals.

Additionally, there are some skeletal individuals who I have become acquainted with through their bones and they have gained my respect for the pain they must have endured or the hardships that came their way. Some populations gain my respect for their ingenuity in artifact manufacture or the evidence that they took care of their elderly, injured, or sick. Hence, my respect does not involve a spiritual connection rather it comes from the knowledge that can be gained from studying these remains. The respect comes from knowing what can be learned from studying bones; in other words, knowing their true values. And I hope other scholars respect human remains for similar reasons.

In addition, like a forensic anthropologist studying a crime victim seeks to give the victim a voice, I hope to give whole populations a chance to tell their stories. I want to be able to understand what life was like for these peoples. I want to know where they came from; were they still adapted to the Ice Ages as the hip bone indicates in Kennewick Man or did they arise from Australia as the Lucia skeleton dated to 12,000 years found in South America. Who fought for resources and how were the peoples affected by their environment; today we are concerned about global warming, but their concerns manifested themselves in warfare and battle for water and food. I want to get to know these individuals.

Anthropologist Dr. Philip Walker, who has made a career of studying prehistoric skeletal remains and reconstructing the prehistory of coastal California, in the 2006 book entitled *Biological Anthropology and Ethics* emphasizes the importance of ethics and respect, but he does so without forgetting the anthropologists' duty. He clearly points out that anthropologists, in general, think that bones should be treated ethically and have a high degree of respect for these remains. He makes it clear that the respect is gained through the knowledge of the information that the skeletal remains hold for anthropologists. Our ethical code, which evolved from this respect, Walker states needs to include the preservation of remains in order to be able to gain a greater understanding about the remains. By reburying human remains, we lose the capability to learn more about our past and disrespect the past people by destroying their ability to tell their story.

The respect Native Americans have for the human remains is not necessarily a false form of respect, but I doubt that it comes from valuing the human remains for what they can tell us. For them, the respect is a religious one that is bound by faith rather than inquiry. A Native American interviewed by Nani Ratnawati, a recent graduate of the San Francisco State University Master's Program, clearly points out that respect involves the acceptance of the creation story; "For Rick, a respectful archaeologist is one who does not dismiss Native beliefs." This respect is engrained in them through their culture; have the remains earned the respect in the opinion of the Native Americans? Or rather is it the type of respect expected without a true sense of reverence.

Chapter 4

NAGPRA

"NAGPRA's definition of cultural affiliation is deceptively simple….The categories of evidence recognized in the law as viable to prove cultural affiliation reflect congressional intent to empower Native American groups to assert claims using a broad variety of information."

Susan B. Bruning (2006: Complex Legal Legacies: The Native American Graves Protection and Repatriation Act, Scientific Study, and Kennewick Man. American Antiquity 71).

INTRODUCTION TO NAGPRA

NAGPRA stands for the Native American Graves Protection and Repatriation Act. This act was passed in 1990 as a federal law that requires all federally funded institutions to give affiliated tribes the ability to claim human remains and artifacts for repatriation and reburial. Any museum or other institute that receives money from the federal government is required to comply with NAGPRA. NAGPRA also includes sections on unclaimed and culturally unidentifiable human remains in order to determine affiliation or prevent repatriation to an unaffiliated tribe. Even with this protection, collections of Australian Aborigines housed at the University of California in Los Angeles have been claimed by Native Americans through NAGPRA and are under legal limbo until issues are resolved. Thus, NAGPRA's default is that the Indians are correct in their tagging of remains and the scientists have to show otherwise, even when the remains are obviously not of Native American descent! Federal grants are provided through NAGPRA to Native Americans and the institutions to help with compliance. NAGPRA has penalties for noncompliance and illegal trafficking of materials and remains.

The process of repatriation through NAGPRA follows several steps. First, the institutions have to identify the items (artifacts and human remains) in their possession that are subject to NAGPRA regulations. These institutions prepare an inventory for publication by the Federal Register of the Secretary of the Interior. Next, we have to consult with any possible lineal descendents who contact us after they have examined the inventory from the NAGPRA website or publications. Then, federally recognized lineal descendents can make a claim for repatriation.

Disposition is another caveat on NAGPRA that deals with recently discovered remains. When an excavation occurs on federal or tribal land and human remains or artifacts are found, these may be given to an affiliated tribe even without being put first into the possession of a museum or university.

NAGPRA only deals with federally recognized tribes. This is basically any Native American tribe with land claims and it applies to about 770 tribes listed in the Bureau of Indian Affairs. Nonfederally recognized tribes do not have the right to claim artifacts or remains through NAGPRA. However, there are state laws that include nonfederally recognized tribes, which I will talk about a little later.

Affiliation, which is the term for descendent in repatriation laws, is loosely defined in NAGPRA. The act states that "cultural affiliation" means that "there is a relationship of shared group identity which can be reasonably traced historically or prehistorically between a present day Indian tribe or Native Hawaiian organization and an identifiable earlier group." By using the term cultural affiliation, NAGPRA avoids requiring a biological link and opens up the doors to arguments based on oral tradition. In addition, by the NAGPRA laws, cultural affiliation is determined by a "preponderance of the evidence based upon geographical, kinship, biological, archaeological, anthropological, linguistic, folkloric, oral traditional, historical, or other relevant information or expert opinion." A preponderance of evidence just means enough evidence that would convince a judge or jury. So, if a judge is likely to believe religious stories rather than biological truths, then there may be affiliation without any genetic link.

Not only have there been issues raised with the term cultural affiliation, but also with the definition of Native American. NAGPRA has Native American defined as

> "Of, or relating to, a tribe, people, or culture that is indigenous to the United States. [25 USC 3001 (9)] Of, or relating to, a tribe, people, or culture indigenous to the United States, including Alaska and Hawaii. [43 CFR 10.2 (d)]."

However, there has been a challenge proposed by Senator John McCain of Arizona to change the "is" into "was," so that any remains that are found in the United States that are prehistoric would fall under NAGPRA laws. In part, this attempt to redefine Native American is a backlash from the Kennewick Man struggle. It took 10 years to finally decide that Kennewick Man would not be repatriated since the remains did not fall under the current definition of NAGPRA, but if the word "is" were to be changed to "was," then the opportunity to claim such ancient Americans would be strengthened. This issue will be addressed again since the proposition has recently resurfaced.

HISTORY OF REPATRIATION AND REBURIAL LAWS IN THE US

NAGPRA was one of the last federal laws to help protect Native Americans. There were a series of laws starting in 1906 that dealt with Native American issues. First, Congress passed the Antiquities Act of 1906 to stop the looting of Native American sites. Then, in 1978, the American Indian Religious Freedom Act passed, which put Native American religion on the same footing as other recognized religions. And, in 1988, the Archaeological Resources Protection Act was passed, which was used to protect artifacts. This law made it illegal to remove Native American artifacts from government land without a permit. Furthermore, once an item was removed it stated that it should be preserved in a suitable institution and not repatriated.

The repatriation movement started long before it was passed by the George Bush Sr. administration in 1990. Prior to 1970s, most people gave little thought to prehistoric remains in the USA. The public changed their minds around 1976 when Maria Pearson, a Yankton-Sioux Native American from Iowa, found out that a road crew had excavated a gravesite. This excavation unburied 26 white skeletons and only one female Native American skeleton. Iowa state officials reburied the white people's bones in a new cemetery, but the Indian remains were not reburied, but rather passed on to an institution to be studied. Maria Pearson claimed that this was discrimination against Native Americans. And, as Pearson, Native American tribes, and others fought for the civil rights of Native American human remains, a wave of support grew that ended in the enactment of NAGPRA in 1990.

In 1986, the Cheyenne tribe became engaged in the repatriation and reburial movement when they discovered the Smithsonian housed 18,500 human remains. Between 1986 and 1990, they organized tribes across the continent in an effort to pass legislation to repatriate remains. They were successful in getting state and federal laws passed to remove museum and university collections. The 1980s were marked with tribes seeking to take remains out of institutions and rebury them; for example, anthropologist Nani Ratnawati discusses the Larsen Bay tribal council resolution that was asking for the return of human remains as early as 1987. In 1989, the National Museum of the American Indian Act was passed that required the first large repatriation and reburial to take place. This act was only imposed on the Smithsonian and it basically required museum officials to inventory and publish the remains housed in the institute for consideration of repatriation.

Right before NAGPRA was passed, some museums and universities felt the pressure to repatriate human remains and artifacts to local Indian tribes (Stanford University was one that I mention later in this book). Harvard also caved into the political atmosphere and repatriated human remains and artifacts. Arizona State Museum and Santa Fe's Museum drafted their own repatriation policies and gave away a great deal of data.

Not all anthropologists were on side with repatriation. Many organizations (such as the Society for American Archaeology, the American Association of Physical Anthropology, and the American Anthropological Association) started to consider the effects of repatriation on their scientific activities. Nani Ratnawati pointed out that some academics stated that the living must come before the dead; while others lamented the loss of data. Still others, such as Dr. Clement Meighan, who worked at University of California, Los Angeles and passed away in 1997, talked about the violation of scientific freedom on inquiry even before NAGPRA was passed. Regardless of positions, the path to repatriation had been set and there was little doubt that anthropological research would be affected.

Anthropologists, such as Drs. Douglas Ubelaker and Lauryn Grant in a 1989 *Yearbook of Physical Anthropology* article, point out that European American skeletons have been reburied and, thus, Native Americans have the right to rebury their ancestors. Yet, there have been many Caucasian and other non-white skeletal populations that have not been reburied and continue to be studied. My own work has covered autopsy collections, such as the Terry and Maxwell Collections that include whites and blacks, and Quebec prisoners of war from the 18th-century. The 18th-century prisoners came to light in 1986 when the Canadian Park Services were restoring part of the historic Quebec Wall. Construction workers discovered 50 skeletons that archaeologists dated between 1745 and 1748 AD. These white remains have been made available for study and anthropologists, such as Dr. Jerry Cybulski the curator of the Canadian Museum of Civilization and myself, have used these remains for a good many articles and as a useful comparative sample to other populations. These individuals were white Canadians and Americans from the English region of Canada who had been captured by French Canadians in the French-English war of 1744. The prisoners examined in this study died while under French control. James Richardson, the curator of anthropology at the Carnegie Museum of Natural History, also makes the point that excavations have been carried out on Revolutionary War and Civil War battlefields and the remains of whites found have been studied and not reburied. It is not just Native American remains that scientists are interested in; it is just they are the most abundant human remains here in the United States. As I said before, if I lived in Europe, I would be studying European remains.

STRANGE BEDFELLOWS: HOW NAGPRA WAS PASSED

Although Native Americans were at the forefront of repatriation and reburial fights for legislation, it would be naïve to think that they were alone in the fight to pass reburial laws. NAGPRA was not passed purely due to the efforts of Native Americans, but rather a consortium of peoples helped to pass NAGPRA. Some of these individuals would rather never be in the same room with one another and yet they helped pass a law that would change the way anthropology is conducted forever. Native Americans alone did not have the political power to create or enforce NAGPRA. In getting NAGPRA enacted, they received help from some very unlikely allies, including agencies of the government, Christian fundamentalists, and liberal activists.

In 1997, Douglas Preston pointed out that the US Army Corps of Engineers and the US Department of the Interior supported the passing of NAGPRA mainly out of concern for access to land and water rights considered essential for the development of hydroelectric power projects, dams, and toxic waste dumps. If you take a look at the land that has been determined to be Native American land by the Indian Claim's Commission, which was established in 1946 to settle land claim disputes between Native Americans and the US government, you can see that the Native American land and where military bases are located overlap a great deal (Figure 13). The locations of the Southwest, Northwest, Southeast, and the Great Lake region are all areas that have a great deal of Native American land and large military bases; Florida, Arizona, and Washington are also great examples of this overlap. I suspect that the US government did not pass NAGPRA just to undo wrongs that occurred in the past, but rather had a stake in giving some power to Native Americans in order to ease tensions due to shared lands. The rumors of government motive were rife in the Kennewick Man case. For example, Alan Schneider the lawyer for the scientists in the Kennewick Man lawsuit claimed that Army Corps of Engineers may need to have tribal support because of dams on the Columbia and Snake rivers. Another theory, published in the *Willamette Week* April 22nd 1998 by journalist Maureen O'Hagan, is that the corps had plans for chemical weapons storage at the Umatilla weapons depot. In many cases, the government collaboration with Native Americans occurs only where resources (particularly natural resources) are at stake.

Indian Land Areas Judicially Established 1978

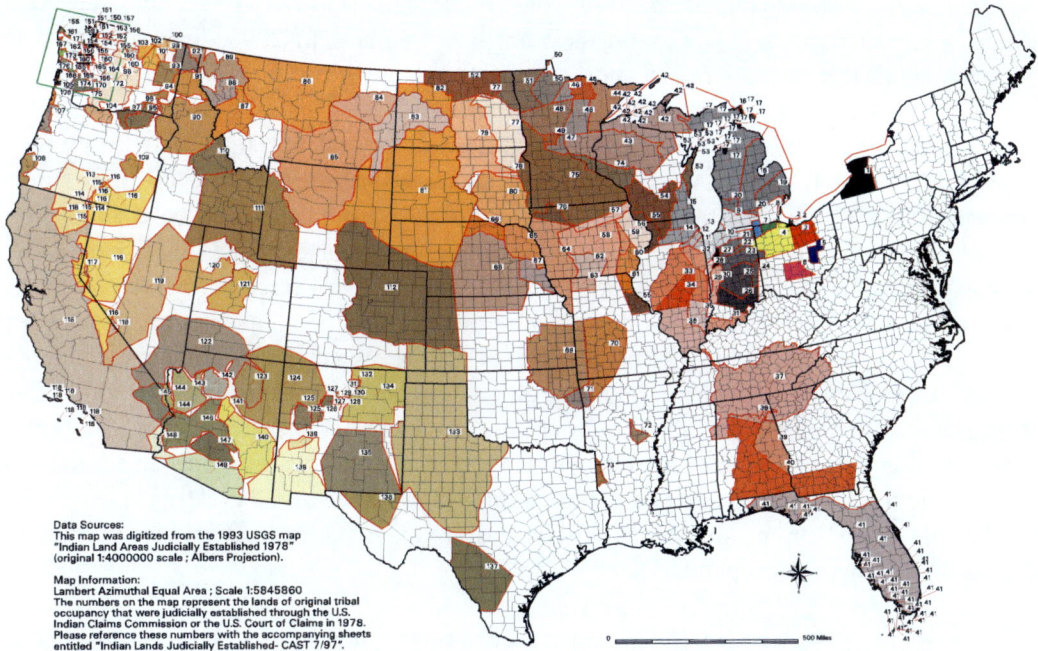

Data Sources:
This map was digitized from the 1993 USGS map
"Indian Land Areas Judicially Established 1978"
(original 1:4000000 scale ; Albers Projection).

Map Information:
Lambert Azimuthal Equal Area ; Scale 1:5845860
The numbers on the map represent the lands of original tribal
occupancy that were judicially established through the U.S.
Indian Claims Commission or the U.S. Court of Claims in 1978.
Please reference these numbers with the accompanying sheets
entitled "Indian Lands Judicially Established- CAST 7/97".

Military Bases in the Continental United States

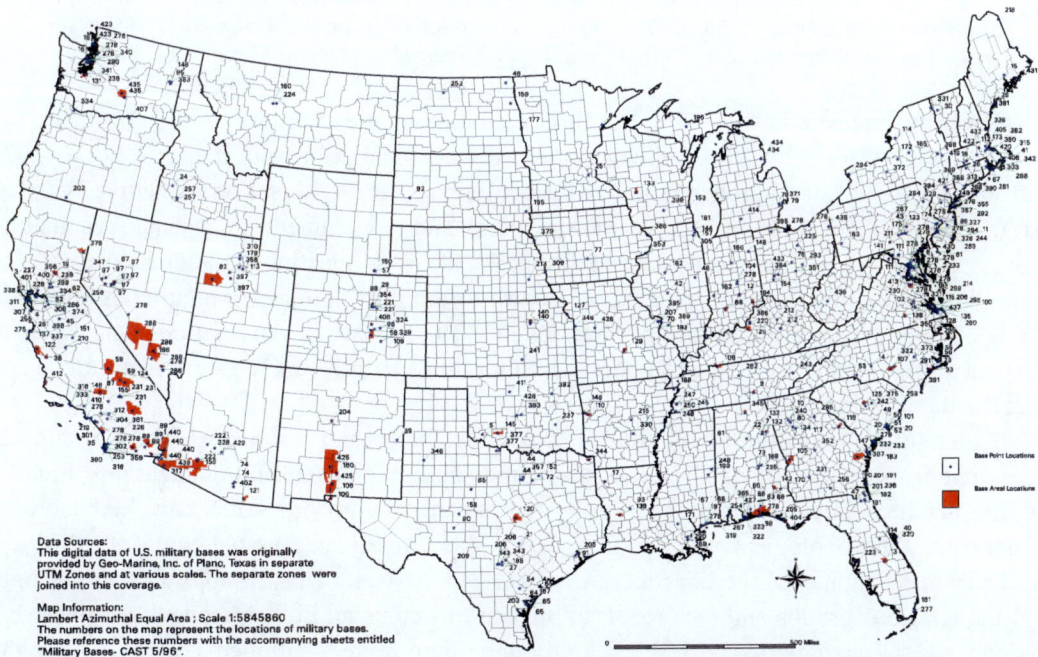

Data Sources:
This digital data of U.S. military bases was originally
provided by Geo-Marine, Inc. of Plano, Texas in separate
UTM Zones and at various scales. The separate zones were
joined into this coverage.

Map Information:
Lambert Azimuthal Equal Area ; Scale 1:5845860
The numbers on the map represent the locations of military bases.
Please reference these numbers with the accompanying sheets entitled
"Military Bases- CAST 5/96".

Figure 13. These maps demonstrate the overlap of Native American lands with military bases. The top map shows Indian Reservations wherever there is red, the bottom shows the military bases in green. Note the high density areas that overlap in the two maps on both coasts. These maps are provided free to the public by the Department of the Interior.

Churches were more than pleased to inhibit explanations of human origins via evolution. The Mennonites were and still are a strong voice in the support of NAGPRA. They repeatedly publish repatriation success stories on their on-lines journals. In 2006, they supported the Cheyenne in their repatriation demands as evidenced by the Mennonite Heritage Center Calendar. The support for the return of sacred bones to sacred land by the Mennonite (and other religious organizations) should not surprise academics. Just as Native American religion is anti-scientific and Native American claims to know their origins via creation stories, Christian groups follow the Bible and do not wish their creation myths to be challenged by modern scientific endeavors. Under the Mennonite religion, for example, they "believe that God has created human beings." They also believe that "God has created the heavens and the earth and all that is in them." With these strong biblical beliefs, archaeological evidence of evolution is deemed as useless. The Church of Christ, Evangelical Lutheran Church in America, Church of the Bretheren, and the others all support a literal interpretation of the bible along with shunning scientific evidence for evolution. Consequently, supporting NAGPRA was a way to seem liberal and support a liberal agenda while also squashing scientific inquiry into times prior to 5,000 to 6,000 years, which would greatly challenge their beliefs. This overwhelming support from religious groups is pointed out by Drs. C. Timothy McKeown and Sherry Hutt in their 2003 article:

"A May 11, 1990 letter to House and Senate members urging passage of repatriation legislation was signed by representatives of the American Baptist Churches, American Ethical Union, Church of the Bretheren, Church Women United, Evangelical Lutheran Church in America, Friends Committee on National Legislation, Episcopal Church, Jesuit Social Ministries, Mennonite Central Committee, Presbyterian Church, Unitarian Universalist Association of Congregations, United Church of Christ, and the United Methodist Church."

Other examples of how religion has supported the repatriation movement comes from Dr. Kathleen Fine-Dare's 2002 book *Grave Injustice* where she points out that as early as 1971 the World Council of Churches organized a conference on the liberation of Native Peoples. At this conference, anthropologists, missionaries, and government representatives met to discuss all sorts of indigenous issues. Additionally, at recent meetings to address the issue of reburying unidentified human remains, A Return to the Earth project (which is an operation made of over 70 faith-based groups) has taken a strong part in repatriation. One issue of particular importance was that of freeing the cultural properties from Western institutions and repatriating human remains.

Letters of support from other sides of the political spectrum emerged. A letter of support also came from the American Civil Liberties Union and several Jewish organizations. Finally, adding insult to injury, academic groups, such as the Society for American Archaeology, American Anthropological Association, and the American Association of Physical Anthropology, supported the enactment of NAGPRA as well. Thus, it appears that not only did the religious groups embrace repatriation, but museums and other academics underwent change and also supported NAGPRA (although there were continued concerns over the repatriation of very ancient remains and strongholds in the academic community who were aghast at the loss of scientific data).

So, left-wing activists concerned with minority and aboriginal rights joined the right-wing creationists, the Army, and the government and thereby proving that politics does indeed sometimes make for strange bedfellows. It was this unusual alliance of liberal activists and conservative creationists that helped pass NAGPRA.

WHAT NAGPRA COVERS: WHO GETS WHAT BONES

NAGPRA and other state laws, which are discussed later, do not account for unaffiliated remains. This is the saving grace of NAGPRA and should be held to its strictest guidelines. But, affiliation even in the strictest sense is loosely defined as it can be determined through science, culture, or religion. Regardless, there are remains that are determined as unaffiliated. Instead of using these remains for study, some states have required the reburial of even these remains while other states and organizations have fought to have these remains included in NAGPRA. An article written by Lillian Thomas for the *Pittsburgh Post-Gazette* highlights this issue. Thomas starts off by stating:

> "On a ridge outside Morgantown, W.Va., work has stopped on a shopping mall while archaeologists excavate human remains found last month in an area where a group of Monongahela Indians once lived.
>
> The remains are orphans, in a sense. There is no modern-day Monongahela tribe, and clear traces of the group disappear from the archaeological record before the arrival of European settlers."

She quotes many Native Americans who use religious arguments against the value of scientific study. She also points out that while NAGPRA and other state laws are worked out to deal only with affiliated remains, "some museums and other institutions contacted tribes that might hold cultural links with materials they have, and, in many cases, went ahead with repatriation." This is what occurred in Morgantown with the remains she wrote about. How can scientists cave into Native American religion and repatriate bones that they could use for scientific study? Even if Native Americans claim they already know their history, doesn't the past belong to everyone?

NAGPRA also does not cover remains that are in private institutions (those in private collections that do not receive any federal funding) or disposition of remains found on private lands. However, some state laws cover the issue of human remains found on private property. In a nutshell, NAGPRA covers federally recognized tribes, anything found on Indian Reservations, and anything found on government land.

PROBLEMS WITH NAGPRA

One of the major problems with NAGPRA and other repatriation laws is their focus on giving legitimacy to oral traditions. By allowing oral traditions to be evidence for affiliation, the lawmakers have created a tug of war between scientists and Native Americans. Oral traditions are not evidence of biological affiliation. In *Mammoth Trumpet's* June 2001 issue anthropologist Dr. Harry Glenn Custred highlighted some of the problems with oral tradition. He starts off by pointing out that scholars have long been trying to dissect oral traditions in order to gain some facts from them, but that it usually ends up in bitter disputes between the scientists and the cultures they are studying. Scholars are often surprised at how similar oral traditions of unrelated groups are, which suggests that people put stuff in their oral traditions to suit their purposes. Also, unlike legends, oral traditions and folklore often have no historical or prehistorical validity pertaining to the truth; the oral traditions of alien abductions in New Mexico have just as much validity as the creation myths of the Native Americans. One creation myth, reported by Jeffrey Kluger and Dan Cray in a 2006 article in *Time* magazine and was stated by Rochanne Downs coordinator of Great Basin tribes, is that "Our people were made from mud, and then the tribes were sent out." Others, such as the Mojave of California believe that people lived underground in the beginning of time and when their food diminished, they sent a hummingbird to the surface to search for more. The bird found a lot of food, and then the people climbed out of the ground and moved into this new world.

One example of the lack of legitimacy to oral traditions has been highlighted by anthropologist Dr. John Ewer who looked at the introduction of the horse in Blackfoot Indians based in Montana. There is strong historical evidence that the horse was brought to North America in the 1700s and reached the Blackfoot's territory around the middle of that century. These dates are documented and have been repeatedly found to be replicable through the study of various historical papers. However, Dr. Ewer asking the Blackfoot Indians today found a different story. They gave Ewer several myths; one of which included that the horse was given to their tribes by the gods of Thunder or Morning Star. Some myths even state that the horse was created by gods for the European visitors. This example demonstrates how a known event can be transmuted by myths and have no legitimacy. Their only value may be for cultural anthropologists who are interested in religion and mythology. If this is the type of evidence is used for repatriation, scientific endeavors to prove no affiliation are useless. Also, surprisingly, there are anthropologists who take seriously the Native American accounts of their prehistory. They accept the Native American beliefs and give legitimacy to stories, which deserve none, while other anthropologists have concerned themselves with only valid evidence to reconstruct the past.

Additionally, much of the mythology lacks any written record to support any cultural continuity or true traditional links to past tribes. For example, some groups that have been extremely successful in reburial actions, such as the leaders of Hui Malama I Na Kupuna of Hawaii who have reburied around 6,000 skeletal individuals, have little to no written evidence of their folklore. They have been criticized for rushing reburials in order to avoid other peoples from claiming affiliation and, as well, professor Kanahele of the University of Hawaii a Native Hawaiian herself, has failed to find evidence for reburial requirement. In regards to the reburial practices and folklore that is being used for repatriation in Hawaii by the Malama, Kanahele stated in January 2006 in the *Honolulu Advertiser* that "There's nothing written in a book. It is bogus. They're making it up as they go along."

Even when the oral traditions are not mutated intentionally, there will always be changes to the stories. That is, since oral tradition is not written, the stories often change over time. Things are omitted, added, and fused over the years. Just think about how rumors change over the course of a couple of days, when things are not written down, they don't stay constant. I could tell my sister a story today and she could pass it onto her friend the next day, and it would have already changed. Now multiply these changes by thousands of people and over hundreds of generations. The stories must change. On Friends of America's Past website it states that "oral narratives are extremely mutable, and are unlikely to retain any historical accuracy after even 500 to 1000 years." Putting this in perspective to some controversial human remains, Kennewick Man and Spirit Cave, both of which have faced NAGPRA's reburial threat, are older than 8,000 years. The Pauite Indians have just recently lost one battle against the reburial of Spirit Cave. The Federal government has ruled that being prehistoric is not enough to make a find Native American (this same ruling applied to Kennewick Man and saved him from reburial) and unless more evidence is provided to prove that Spirit Cave is affiliated with the tribe, Spirit Cave man will be free for scientific study. Interestingly, the Pauite tried to use oral tradition as their secondary evidence. They state that since their oral tradition contains no mention of migration or other Indians speaking other languages the Spirit Cave mummy must be related. The Spirit Cave evidence was nearly identical to that of Kennewick Man where oral tradition was used by the Native Americans to attempt to claim affiliation of the 9,300 year-old skeleton. The evidence was extremely weak with the Native Americans claiming that their oral traditions provided enough evidence that no migrations occurred and that they had been there since the beginning of time. There is no evidence that these myths are accurate; rather there is a growing mountain of evidence that the oral traditions of most Native Americans are in fact false. This is true for other claims, especially in regards to the oldest Native Americans, such as Spirit Cave Man.

In summary, oral traditions cannot stand the pressure of time. NAGPRA officials are clearly aware of this due to anthropologists who have reported of the lack of consistency in oral traditions over time. For example, in the American Association of Physical Anthropologists Newsletter, in the summer of 2003, anthropologists Andre Simic from the University of Southern California in Los Angeles, and Harry Glenn Custred, Jr., from the California State University, are cited as scientists who addressed the Department of Interior's use of oral traditions to support cultural affiliation in the Kennewick Man case. They both stated that folklore and oral traditions "are unlikely to retain any historical accuracy after 500 to 1000 years." Further, they mentioned that the creation stories told by the Umatillas are myths and that "myths are the least factually reliable type of oral tradition." On the other hand, they are the most commonly used type of oral tradition by Native Americans when trying to repatriate human remains. Dr. Geoffrey Clark, a paleoanthropologist at Arizona State University, laments the use of oral traditions in NAGPRA. In a 1999 article he wrote in the *Skeptical Inquirer* he states that:

> "Laws like NAGPRA strike at the heart of scientific archaeology because they elevate Indian cultural traditions and religious beliefs to the level of science of a paradigm for describing or explaining reality."

The use of oral traditions is extremely troublesome in NAGPRA since they provide no real evidence of continuity and, therefore, affiliation. If the use of oral tradition continues, it should at least be done with rigor of other evidence considered. Can you imagine other laws that would require only myths to support their claims? Of course, Native Americans feel very different from scientists about oral traditions. For example, the Denver repatriation coordinator Roger Echo-Hawk insists that tribal memories do indeed stretch to the dawn of time.

Another problem with NAGPRA has been highlighted by the Society for American Archaeology; this problem is the increase in dealing with culturally unidentifiable human remains. NAGPRA was originally intended to deal with culturally identifiable remains and stated that other types of human remains should be kept at the institutions that housed them. In recent years, many museums and universities have requested NAGPRA reviews in order to know what to do with the unaffiliated or unidentified remains. Some institutions face a great deal of pressure from Native American groups and others to rid their institutions of all human remains. The Society for American Archaeology claims that this has caused the "illegal broadening of the concept of cultural affiliation" and "bears directly on treatment of so-called culturally unidentifiable human remains," which are human remains that that cannot be culturally affiliated with any living tribe.

In the original NAGPRA laws, institutions were required to complete inventories of all remains and then keep the unaffiliated and unidentified remains in their custody. By having these inventories complete, however, the institutes are open to being harassed by groups requesting reburials and the institutions request that they be allowed to repatriate all human remains to tribal consortia. These decisions occur most often without scientific approval or even input from the local anthropological communities. Society for American Archaeology suggests that culturally unidentifiable remains not be inventoried or reburied. What has occurred instead is that the institutions seek special reviews in order to rebury these remains too. Furthermore, NAGPRA officials most often give the institutions the okay to rebury these remains.

Dealing with culturally unaffiliated and unidentifiable remains has been an issue with NAGPRA. Anthropologists have consistently pointed out to federal legislators and Native Americans that NAGPRA's intent was not to deal with unaffiliated and unidentifiable remains. There is no definition of unaffiliated or unidentifiable in NAGPRA. Dr. Tim White, curator of the Phoebe Hearst Museum at University of California, Berkeley, in a 1999 letter to the NAGPRA review committee points out in regards to culturally unidentifiable human remains that:

> "If congressional intent were to make it possible for Federally recognized tribes to claim culturally unidentifiable human remains on behalf of unrecognized tribes or others, the statute would have so stated."

He further adds that the prevailing attitude that "human remains for which there is little or no information should be speedily repatriated since they have little educational, historical, or scientific value," is harmful to scientific inquiry.

Dr. Fred Smith, the current president of the American Association of Physical Anthropologists, is also concerned with the escalation in repatriation of or talk of repatriation of unaffiliated remains. In a letter to Dr. Sherry Hutt, the NAGPRA National Manager, Smith posted on the American Association of Physical Anthropologists website he states his concerns that:

> "human remains and other cultural items for which a qualified claimant has not been identified based on the provisions of Section 3(a) should be retained in Federal care. Current regulations (36 CFR 79) governing federal curation facilities adequately address issues related to the preservation and handling of human remains and other cultural items for which a qualified claimant has not been identified. Such remains should be retained by the federal government until they are claimed by a qualified party."

Even remains with no provincial information can be useful in understanding the past and present of bone biology and health, how to identify sex and age in fragmentary remains (which can be used in forensics), and much more. Dr. Tim White adds that even if repatriation would occur with these remains, who would they be repatriated to? NAGPRA states that repatriation can only occur to federally recognized and culturally affiliated tribes. Repatriation of these remains would break NAGPRA's laws. Nevertheless, these unaffiliated remains are frequently repatriated.

NAGPRA has been expanding and the determinations of what should be repatriated are becoming looser. NAGPRA's wording is vague and opens up a whole slew of problems. It is most important to remember the initial intent of NAGPRA in order to keep the loss of data to a minimum; that intent was to repatriate ancestral remains to federally recognized affiliated tribes. This isn't about taking all remains and burying them, even though sometimes that is the outcome.

Along this line of concern, one of the scariest developments was the meeting of NAGPRA officials that have started in order to seize unidentified and unaffiliated remains. Although, anthropologists and others have pointed out that these actions counter the original intent of NAGPRA the wave of reburial is proceeding. For example, just this March, NAGPRA meetings occurred in order to discuss unaffiliated remains. According to a 2007 article in the *Native American Times*, the National NAGPRA Office claims that there are around 140,000 unidentified or unaffiliated remains in universities and museums in the United States and the NAGPRA Review Committee has recommended regional cemeteries for these remains.

As if dealing with the above-mentioned problems is not enough to worry scientists, we must also delve into the problem of the definition of Native American. Attorney Alan Schneider wrote about the different interpretations of Native American for the Mammoth Trumpet in 2001, but since then there have been no changes to aid in addressing the meaning of Native American according to federal law. As I mentioned before, Native American is defined in NAGPRA as "of, or relating to, a tribe, people or culture that is indigenous to the United States." Alan Schneider states that "scientists argue that Congress intended NAGPRA to apply to only those remains and objects that are related to existing indigenous peoples." This would make sense since affiliation is required to repatriate remains; however, NAGPRA does not contain this specific temporal reference. So, for scientists, NAGPRA should not be applicable to remains that are not related to an existing tribe. The government, Schneider writes, has a different interpretation. Its argument is that NAGPRA doesn't need a relationship to present-day peoples. Basically, they seem to define Native American as anything prior to the arrival of Europeans and, therefore, remains even as old as Kennewick Man need to be dealt with through the federal government law. Native Americans, as reported by the National Congress of American Indians, have the same interpretation as the government. Schneider points out that the scientists' interpretation is more in line with the intent of NAGPRA, which was to return remains that were ancestral to modern peoples. With the scientists' interpretation, we could at least keep on studying remains that had no present day affiliated group. However, the scientists' interpretation is the one that is most often faulted and, thus, remains are being repatriated with real affiliation or not.

Another issue with NAGPRA is their lack of addressing the need for scientific study. Even though NAGPRA does not prohibit scientific study, such as some state laws, it provides no requirement of a scientific study either. Human remains need to be studied even if they will be reburied eventually. By not requiring scientific study, oral traditions may be the only evidence. The scientific community deserves at least the same amount of authority as the Native American community. If we must have a NAGPRA law, then it must be more specific in the requirement or at least the allowance of scientific study.

Therefore, even with the victories of Kennewick Man and Spirit Cave, anthropologists have much reason to be concerned at the number of remains that are being lost to the study of science. But, not only are federal legislative actions of concern, but state laws as well have expanded reburial and loosened requirements for repatriation.

Chapter 5

STATE LAWS

"California bill (AB 978), that is designed to empty the museums at the whim of Indian groups in California. Not satisfied with the results of NAGPRA they have crafted a bill, that besides likely transgressing federal and state takings provisions, allows any Indian group federally recognized or not, to walk into any museum and remove ANY object from the shelves and take them away."

M. Steven Shackley
(2001: Letter to Friends of America's Past).

SPREAD OF REPATRIATION AND REBURIAL: NAGPRA IS NOT ENOUGH

Many states have their independent laws to help Native American tribes repatriate remains. These laws have come both before and after NAGPRA. Dr. Kathleen Fine-Dare points out that in 1989 Nebraska enacted the Unmarked Human Burial Sites and Skeletal Remains Protection Act. This was the first law in the country that required museums to return all Native American bones that could be affiliated with living tribes and became the model for NAGPRA. The intersection of these state laws and federal laws has been problematic to many anthropologists. Some of the laws are much less stringent in regards to determining affiliation than NAGPRA whereas others are more so. Some state laws directly contradict federal laws, such as in California where the law requires repatriation of remains to affiliated groups even without federal recognition, but NAGPRA makes it illegal to dispose of remains to nonfederally recognized tribes. New Jersey and Alaska are the only two states without repatriation and reburial laws. Alaska, nonetheless, does have a Historic Preservation Act that covers Native American remains. Most state laws were passed or amended within 5 years of NAGPRA being passed.

Most states laws allow for scientific study of human remains if the remains are of importance to the state or country; how importance is determined is never clear. With all states that allow scientific study, the time limits can be severe with the longest period of time being one year, like in Maine and Montana, but many have one month or six month limits, like Kansas and Arizona, which can lead to the inability to conduct many types of research. Furthermore, some states require tribal consultation prior to the possibility of study or even tribal supervision of the scientists, such as in Indiana. Oklahoma requires consultation with tribal leaders in order to ask for permission to do an initial study of human remains. There are some states that do not allow any study, such as Arkansas and Indiana, if affiliation can be determined without studying the bones. In addition, some states will rebury or place remains off limits to scientists even if no claims by Native Americans have been made. Arizona requires museums to rebury or store remains without study if no claims have been made by tribes within 6 months. What's more, Arizona law requires that even remains with no cultural affiliation to modern populations be reburied. Thus, even when remains are not being requested, they cannot be kept by the universities of the state! All state laws require repatriation or reburial whether or not a scientific study has been conducted and most often the costs are on the anthropologists' institutions. I will highlight California's laws below.

California passed a law called CalNAGPRA (AB978) in 2001 that removes the requirement of Federal recognition for Native American groups who are culturally affiliated (which is broadly defined and can be proven with no scientific evidence) to obtain human remains. CalNAGPRA has formed a commission appropriately entitled the Repatriation Oversight Commission. This Commission had its first meeting on February 12, 2004 when they established a list of nonfederally recognized tribes in California. This list has now been prepared and the law will begin to take effect. By Dr. Fine-Dare's assessment "California has one of the most 'sweeping and severe' burial laws of any state in the nation, legislation that applies to both public and private property."

How does CalNAGPRA affect anthropology? First, CalNAGPRA allows as much weight to be given to Native American's "oral histories" and "tribal testimonies" as to forensic, geological, or other scientific evidence when determining affiliation. This is clear in its section:

> "Tribal oral histories, documentations, and testimonies shall not be afforded less evidentiary weight than other relevant categories of evidence on account of being in those categories."

The requirement for preponderance of evidence for affiliation, in consequence, may weigh only on the Native American evidence. In California, scientists are required to disprove the Native American traditions in order to prevent reburial. This makes scientists the bad guys again and makes it nearly impossible for scientists to avoid the loss of data. After all, one cannot prove that something did not occur; we can only prove things are present, not absent. So, to require scientists to disprove religious stories is unreasonable. We cannot prove that there is no God or that the creation myths are not true. Rather we can show that the human remains in possession and the modern tribes are either similar or different to a specific statistic degree, which confers certainty. For example, we can say with 95% certainty that Kennewick Man and modern Native Americans are morphologically dissimilar; that is, they do not look alike. The Native Americans can still come back with their traditions and state that people have changed and their religion is proof enough to prove the necessary link. The conflict between the scientists and the Native Americans is increased through poorly written and biased laws, such as CalNAGPRA.

CalNAGPRA also singles out geographic location as enough reasonable evidence for affiliation. If a tribe is located in a spot where remains are currently found, then they can be considered affiliated. This totally ignores the fact that people have been moving around for millions of years. Our first trip out of Africa was at least 1.78 million years ago. We have never been a sedentary animal and, thus, equating location with affiliation is absurd. NAGPRA, at least, only uses location to establish the current group identity rather than the link to the past.

Another problem is that CalNAGPRA does not try to make any provisions for unaffiliated remains. Basically, the assumption is that all remains can be affiliated and since affiliation can be claimed based on geography or Native American folklore alone, then all remains will be eventually claimed. On the other hand, this may cause Native American tribes to get embroiled in disputes over who are the truly affiliated tribes.

CalNAGPRA applies to public and private institutions in California, which include the entire University of California and California State University systems. This means that these universities are required to comply with two repatriation laws rather than just one. This is problematic because the laws contradict each other. For example, nonfederally recognized tribes can retrieve human remains through CalNAGPRA, but NAGPRA makes it illegal to repatriate remains to nonfederally recognized tribes (which law does one abide by?). In order to be in compliance with both laws, the institution with the remains or artifacts is required to actually make a request for a review by NAGPRA prior to handing over the remains.

CalNAGPRA also has severe penalties attached to noncompliance, which is supposedly how CalNAGPRA will be paid for. Penalties can be up to $20,000 for each act of noncompliance, but violation of California reburial laws are also considered a felony that can be punishable by imprisonment. One factor that determines the severity of the penalty includes the "cultural and spiritual significance of the item involved." As a result, the government is making science pay according to the religious significance of an object or human remains. Additionally, CalNAGPRA has a severely reduced time limit for compliance; within three months, institutions need to be in compliance (which means inventories published on the remains and artifacts and appropriate contacts to Native Americans made). Another difference between NAGPRA and CalNAGPRA is that CalNAGPRA requires the institutions to take actions to contact and help tribes repatriate the remains; whereas, NAGPRA requires the tribes to seek out the collections through the registry.

Most importantly, one section of CalNAGPRA states, "Determination of cultural affiliation shall not be construed to authorize the completion or initiation of any scientific study of human remains or cultural items." In other words, besides determining cultural affiliation, scientists cannot conduct research on the remains while the fate of remains has not been decided. Once cultural affiliation is determined and repatriation processes begin, it may be too late to conduct additional research. This could be the end of California bioarchaeology. Instead, anthropologists will become mere tools for Native Americans to claim the skeletal collections and determine affiliation. Perhaps the penalties could bankrupt archaeological activities as well.

In summary, all reburial laws have embedded in them vague concepts of scientific importance and cultural affiliation. What this means is that non-scientists are determining the scientific importance of finds to rule whether the human remains can be studied and to what extent. Also cultural affiliation is a vague concept of linking the past with the present. These terms are used most often to make reburial and repatriation easier and make scientific study more difficult. It is scary that none of the state laws, or NAGPRA for that matter, requires scientific evidence for affiliation! Some states, such as California, only require the Native American stories for affiliation. And, many laws do not allow study of remains beyond the determination of affiliation. When research is allowed, the time limits are severely limited;

meaning that only a handful of scientists will have access to remains. Furthermore, many states require permission to study remains; this permission is often in consultation with tribes who are mostly against the study of the human remains. Supervision of archaeologists and the requirement of treating remains in manners that are in accord to Native American religious beliefs are also common.

LAWS THAT PREVENT NEW COLLECTIONS TO BE FOUND

Repatriation and reburial usually consists of removing remains curated at museums and universities and giving them to tribal groups. There are, however, laws that prevent the discovery of new sites and the collection of new remains, which means that as more and more remains are repatriated fewer skeletal remains will be available for study. There are state laws that protect unmarked burials and these laws increase in their coverage each year. These laws make it illegal to intentionally disturb human remains and give guidelines as to how to dispose of remains if they are unintentionally discovered. Some of these laws allow for a study period, but most of the study times are minimal and none allow for the legal long-term curation of remains recently discovered.

NAGPRA and state repatriation and reburial laws are the death of American bioarchaeology. With time, there will be no remains to study and new remains exposed will be off limits almost immediately. Our progress in understanding the first Americans has greatly deteriorated already and will continue to do so. Finally, the penalties for not following the laws are steep and costs for repatriation and reburial almost always fall on the scientists. Why should archaeologists pay for funerals of Native Americans who had no funeral the first time around? And, why should they be required to practice religious acts that are not their religion? Finally, how can some states require reburial even without a tribe to claim the remains? How can a progressive country like our own choose religion over science?

Chapter 6

GLOBAL REPATRIATION AND REBURIAL LAWS

"American Indians, Australian aborigines, and ultra-orthodox Jews in Israel have all attacked archaeology in recent years and continue to seek restrictions on archaeological study."

Clement W. Meighan (2003: Burying American Archaeology.
Academic Questions Vol. 6).

GEOGRAPHIC EXPLORATION OF LOSS OF HUMAN REMAINS: REPATRIATION AND REBURIAL BEYOND THE US

Israel

In 1996, Haim Watzman published on the demise of osteology in Israel. In Israel, orthodox Jews have been waging a bitter battle against archaeologists. They have been trying to stop nearly all excavations, stop the study of human remains, and rebury remains as old as 40,000 years! Israeli anthropologists, such as Dr. Pat Smith, have urged the international academic community to help protect Middle East science. Her plea can be seen on the Friends of America's Past website (www.friendsofpast.com). The chief scientist of the Israel Academy of Sciences and other members of the academy are continually struggling to keep the study of human skeletons alive in Israel, but ultra-orthodox Jews who control part of the government have been focused on stopping the study of human prehistory mainly because it contradicts theological beliefs. Current laws in Israel forbid excavation or analysis of human remains from any period, which includes Neanderthal fossils since the religious factions claim that the world is a mere 6,000 years old. Complaints also have been lodged against universities for conducting research, which resulted in university officials handing over all bones. Yet, the loss of skeletal studies has not been enough for the Jewish orthodox; anthropological research containing evolution and other prehistory topics has been abandoned in universities since 1995! In the January 2000 issue of *Science*, Michael Balter reports on the dismal state of anthropology and reburial in Israel. Basically, ultra-orthodox Jews protest any removal of bones and even orthodox rabbis who have accepted that bones can be removed in digs have insisted that they be reburied without any analysis conducted. This has resulted in the end of physical anthropological studies conducted from Israeli excavations, regardless of whether the excavations are conducted due to construction or for scientific endeavors. Let us only hope that the Native Americans and fundamental Christians do not gain clout and join forces to stop the telling of prehistory in the US.

Australia

At the 2000 American Anthropological Association, Joe Watkins presented the information on global growth of reburial, which highlighted the situation in Australia and New Zealand. In Australia, repatriation and reburial laws have been in motion since the early 1980s. The Australian federal law states that any remains pre-1770 are by definition aboriginal and, therefore, in the control of Aboriginal authorities. The Australian Anthropological Association has been supportive of reburial of later human remains, but points out that the earlier specimens are of scientific importance and should not be destroyed through reburial. However, like in the United States, claims for earlier and earlier remains are being made. Interestingly, Dr. Robyne Bancroft, an aboriginal archaeologist at Australia National University, pointed out that Australian aborigines accept the 60,000 year date for the arrival of humans on the island and claim a direct lineage from that date. Fortunately, they are also more likely to be in favor of some scientific analyses and have even adopted the date of their arrival (60,000 years ago) from the scientific literature. Anthropologists, still, argue that remains that are ancient belong to the world and show no true evidence of direct lineage to modern Aborigines.

The demand for repatriation in Australia recently has taken on a less friendly aura. Repatriation is common now in Australia; Marilyn Truscott, who is the past president for the International Council on Monuments and Sites, (which is closely tied with UNESCO and concerned with preservation of the past) wrote about various reburials that have taken place since 2000. For example, in 2003, 300 human remains were returned to South Australia's native peoples and in that same year the Queensland government passed laws recognizing that Aborigines as the guardians and keepers of their cultural heritage (including artifacts and human remains). The head curator of the National Museum of Australia in 2003, Francesca Cubillo, even wrote a paper called "'Give it Back You Bastards': Indigenous Perspectives on Repatriation of Human remains" to highlight the animosity felt towards anthropologists and the perceived lack of speed in returning aborigine bones. The National Museum of Australia has repatriated most of their remains to aboriginal tribes; over 400 individuals were returned in 2002 and 2003. The following two years the museum turned over nearly 1000 individuals. They have only 28 individuals left in their care, which could still be repatriated. As a result, anyone wishing to conduct osteological studies on the collections can no longer do so.

Intriguingly, remains can only be repatriated if the communities have lands for reburial; hence, much of reburial has been accompanied with the government reserving and giving land to aborigine communities that was once part of the public park system in Australia. Dr. Bancroft wrote in 'Everything Relates, or a Holistic Approach to Aboriginal Indigenous Cultural Heritage' that "land is the overriding issue to Aboriginal people." Aborigines and the Australian government both agree that indigenous communities must have land before they can remove the remains from the universities and other educational institutions. Therefore, we must ask whether they have determined that reburial requests are another way to seize land.

Australian Aborigines have not stopped at their coasts, but have also made requests for return of remains abroad, such those housed in the United Kingdom, Sweden, USA, France, and Germany. In fact, Sweden has repatriated all Australian indigenous human remains housed in their institutions. In addition, the Australian government is requesting inventories from 51 institutions in 13 countries, which include 21 institutions in the United Kingdom, 11 in the USA, seven in Germany, three in Switzerland, two in France, and one in the Czech Republic according to records from Australia's Office of Indigenous Policy Coordination. They state that the objectives are to obtain inventories of Australian Aborigine remains held at overseas institutions and pursue the repatriation of these remains. Once the remains are returned to Australia, they will be repatriated to aborigine communities for reburial or holding. They will deal with institutions directly, but if the remains are not forth coming, their plans are to take the issue to the governments of the respective countries. Recently in 2006, the United Nations have heard pleas from Rosalba Nattero, who is the Vice Chairperson of the Ecospirituality Foundation and representing Wamba Wamba Nation in Australia's Northwestern region, on the state of human remains in various countries. She is appealing for the return and reburial of aboriginal human remains and artifacts. What is fascinating about the appeal is the word genocide is consistently used; thus, Nattero (and presumably the aborigines she represents) think of the lack of repatriation as killing of their culture or people. Some overseas museums and other institutions have complied with demands for the repatriation of remains, but others are still holding out.

Europe

Even though European archaeology is usually free of opposition to excavation and analysis of remains, we are starting to see a small minority group who feel differently. That is, Europe is starting to have to deal with reburial issues as well. Partly, the reburial issue arose from awareness of other reburials around the world. Another aspect comes from Britain's excavation of cemeteries not in use. One 1997 article in *British Archaeology* had quoted Elizabeth Dineley as stating:

"How short a time do we have to be buried before it is permissible, even acceptable, for grinning archaeologists to dig out our bones, prod among our teeth, disperse our possessions, take the head off our horse and lay us, not to rest, in boxes in museums?"

So, the reburial problems of Europe come not only from the demands of foreigners, such as Australian Aborigines and New Zealand Maoris who are asking for remains to be returned to their countries of origin, but also embarrassingly from European pagans. These pagans are demanding reburial of remains and declaring certain archaeological sites as sacred. I am not for repatriation or reburial for these white people either. I personally think that there is virtually no way modern Europeans can claim with any truth to be descendents of very early Europeans since migration and immigration has been rampant; whereas, in Australia and to a lesser degree in the USA, the indigenous groups have been fairly isolated geographically and socially.

Nonetheless, in 2001 anthropologists Robert J. Wallis from the Department of Archaeology at the University of Southampton in England and Jenny Blain from England's Sheffield Hallam University report on the rise in paganism (or nature religions) among modern Europeans and their attempts to foster a reburial movement. These people often claim to be Celtic even if they have no "Scottish, Irish, Cornish, or Manx parentage." This is like some people who claim to be part Native American and have no trace of it in their families. People claiming to be Celtic with no proof state that they know they are Celts; just as religious Native Americans know they were in the Americas since creation. They make claims to have links and deep feelings of connection to prehistoric peoples, such as the Neolithic and Bronze Age groups, and through this connection they want to have sites declared sacred, human remains turned into them, and to stop the scientific accomplishments that help us understand prehistoric Europe. In France, as well, there are some pagan groups who have taken their case to the United Nations last year; the same person who brought the Australian claims to light also represented the Breton community, which is located in France. This community feels it cannot practice its spirituality due to the infringement of archaeology and the preservation of megalithic sites for tourism (such as Stonehenge). They strongly desire to have archaeological sites for their religious practices and I am sure would want to claim any remains or artifacts associated with sites. Should anthropologists take these claims from modern Europeans as serious as other claims from indigenous peoples? Are we looking at the reburial of Otzi the Ice Man or other prehistoric European remains? Drs. Wallis and Blain think:

> "it imperative that the reburial issue in Britain, voiced primarily by Pagans, is examined, as well as guidelines offered which pragmatically address issues of respect and reburial vis-à-vis conservation and academic study."

I would suggest not indulging these people's fantasies of their ancient ancestries and spending more time conducting real scientific research.

Additional European repatriations have occurred in Norway in the late 1990s; Dr. Berit Sellevold participated in reburial of the Saami who are indigenous inhabitant of Norway. Their skulls, which have been repatriated, were collected between 1850 and 1940 and studied by scientists around the world. The Saami view repatriation as a way to right wrongs that have been done to them such as oppression against them by the Norwegian authorities. Religion does not seem to be a theme in their repatriation claims as it is in pagans and Native Americans.

Canada

Canada and US have similar relationships with their majority population and their indigenous populations. As a consequence, it is not surprising that Canada developed similar repatriation legislation for their indigenous populations, who are referred to as First Nations. The Royal Commission on Aboriginal Peoples was established in 1991, shortly after the enactment of NAGPRA, and its policy was to encourage museums and other institutions to engage in voluntary repatriation. The Canadian Museum Association and the Assembly of First Nations established a task force shortly afterward to develop strategies to work together and repatriate artifacts and human remains. In essence, scientific study of human remains is only allowed if individuals from the First Nations approve and are a part of the decision process and prolonged interment of remains is not acceptable. When remains are interred at the museum, First Nation advisors must be consulted in the care for the remains, which involves many of the same demands made by Native Americans. Surprisingly, even remains without an appropriate tribe for repatriation will be reported to the First Nation Assembly, which will decide on the fate of the human remains. In other words, all indigenous remains are at risk for reburial.

Some repatriation cases that have occurred in Canada include Haida reburials. Also, right before the legislation on reburial, in 1989, the first reburials of Sinxt affiliated tribes located in British Columbia occurred and around 61 individuals were lost from science. Furthermore, the Canadian Museum of Civilization, which has an architectural design that is meant to laud the beauty of Native American culture (Figure 14), has had their largest skeletal collections of indigenous populations repatriated and they even paid for the repatriations. For example, "the Museum provided financial and logistical support to the Haida delegation in the repatriation project," which occurred while I was collecting data at the museum for my doctoral dissertation. This included spending money on a feast to show respect, reburial rituals lasting over a week long, and the travel for a large group of Haida to come to the museum. After the Haida had claimed the human remains and had the museum pay for these endeavors, they demanded the destruction of casts of Haida remains. The museum had reached out their hand and yet the Haida still wanted more!

Figure 14. Me in front of the Canadian Museum of Civilization that has been designed to look like a Haida ceremonial mask (2002).

Another unsatisfied group of First Nations, journalist Randy Boswell reports in a 2002 edition of *The Ottawa Citizen*, are the Algonquins. The museum was set to return hundreds of remains to the Algonquins who claim their ancestors inhabited Ottawa for thousands of years. The museum had intended to repatriate all affiliated remains, but the Algonquins wanted even more ancient remains than those that are 5,000 years old. The outcome was that in 2005, all of the demands of the Algonquins were met and even remains as old as 6,000 years were reburied.

WHERE SKELETAL REMAINS HAVE YET TO BE REPATRIATED: ARE THEIR COLLECTION PLACES SAFE?

There are places where anthropological study of human remains continues with little controversy. Europe has begun to have trouble with pagans regarding the reburial of remains, but for the most part these problems are minor compared to that of dealing with indigenous populations' demands. Still, these claims are almost all linked to England and Ireland with some French claims. Other European countries continue to take pride in the study of skeletal material. A flurry of studies has arisen out of Eastern Europe. Poland, Russia, and Croatia have all seen an increase in the study of skeletal remains. Some of these Eastern European countries have started osteological field schools and have been inviting international scholars to study their collections. A quick glance at recent publications in the *American Journal of Physical Anthropology* and the *International Journal of Osteoarchaeology* reveals this renaissance of Eastern European anthropology.

South America has been a haven for anthropologists examining skeletal remains; however, this has begun to change. In his 2001 work, Dr. Gustavo Politis, a professor of archaeology at the Universidad Nacional del Centro in Buenos Aires Argentina, covers some of the highlights of the South American repatriation movement. He highlights the complexities of South American archaeology and claims that it is a colonized science with even the South Americans anthropologists working there merely as agents for North American colonizers. Basically, around the 1980s the American Indians Against Desecration started to make claims on remains in the Americas and Europe; the most successful of their endeavors were in Australia and the USA, but they also encouraged indigenous people throughout the world to voice their opinions on reburial.

In South America, the situation has gained ground, but very slowly and there are no large federal movements to stop scientific activities yet. Dr. Politis sees this as backward and he points out that Australia has had a reburial law since 1984. One of the reasons for the lack of success, according to Politis, is that archaeologists and indigenous groups in South America rarely communicate. Scientists often act without consulting local populations; of course, they are not required to do so either. Another factor concerns the construction of nationalities. Politis claims that the creation of countries has until recently silenced the indigenous populations; that is, in order to have a nationality people had to leave their cultures behind and become Peruvian, Argentinean, etc. With these obstacles, there are some groups that have continued to hang on to their indigenous identities and fought for reburial of remains held in universities and museums. By the early 1980s, Brazil and Bolivia had representatives from indigenous communities making claims for burials to parliament. And, in 1991, Columbia's new constitution had a section respecting indigenous rights and cultural diversity.

Nonetheless, by the 2000s only Peru, Argentina, and Uruguay have standard ways of making claims for the return of human remains from museums and universities. In other countries, there have been no returns or even solicitation from native groups for repatriation of remains. In Argentina, there have been a few claims for repatriation, but these concerned single known historical figures, such as chiefs. What's more, only one of these claims was honored.

However, when remains are older and perhaps of more value, scientists have been successful in continuing excavations, such as Dr. Karl Reinhard from North America who worked with Argentinean students and professors in the excavation of Inca mummies on some of the world's highest Andean mountains. These excavations were successful in retrieving mummies and in part deterring the last remaining mummies from being looted by individuals only interested in monetary profit. The process, yet, was not without its political problems. Gustavo Politis criticizes Reinhard for his National Geographic funding and publications. Furthermore, Politis points out that native peoples took Reinhard to court for not following the regulations; it is important to note that the court found that Reinhard had done nothing wrong and his work continued. Indigenous people claim these mummies should be left in the ground and that the locations are sacred. These modern populations have only an assertion that they are directly related to the mummies whether they are or are not has yet to be determined. Politis does not deem this of importance, rather he concerns himself with the fact that Reinhard and National Geographic are not from South America and do not consult with local populations. Thus, his conclusion is that North America's practice of colonizing extends to the science of anthropology instead of seeing the positive influence the publicity and science has had on the understanding of South America's past. Are today's politics more important than science used to understand the past?

Africa and Asia do not seem to be infected by the repatriation virus that is spreading around the rest of the world. This may change or it could be due in part to the fact that the majority of the skeletal remains in these locations are related to human evolutionary studies rather than prehistory. I shudder to think of the consequences of reburial in Africa if they started to claim that Lucy (the 3.6 million year-old skeleton) should be reburied and the loss of data that would incur. Another fortunate aspect may be that in Africa there is a pride of being the cradle of mankind and also an acknowledgement that these remains can and do increase the world's awareness of the region. These remains also bring much needed funding into African countries and this too aids in the pro-science aura in Africa even though most of the local population is uneducated and not aware of the scientific value of the remains found in their own backyards. Could there be a time when this all changes too? I hope that there are changes; I hope that the changes occur in the level of education and, as a consequence, reduce looting of certain sites. I hope that there does come a day when the local populations are as aware and proud of the evolutionary past that their countries hold as their governments sometimes put forth. And, I hope that they become more and more involved in the study of prehistory and evolution. What I fear is that with knowledge the local populations may wish to kick out Western scientists or that missionaries may be involved in burying the evolutionary past in Africa!

Chapter 7

REPATRIATION AND REBURIAL:
A RELIGIOUS ISSUE

"No doubt religion is the motivator and guide to many members of the public who seek to persuade public officials to adopt policies that comport with their views…With the repatriationist movement, however, governmental policy has adopted and incorporated religious belief and practices. This situation in unique in modern American law, and the courts would not tolerate it in the context of enforcing the majority religion."

Jerry Springer (2005-2006: Scholarship vs. Repatriationism.
Academic Questions Vol. 6)

CREATION STORIES AND SCIENTIFIC INQUIRY

Native American tribes often invoke their creation stories as proof of the unbroken link between the modern tribe and past populations. These creation stories have no foundation in science and, yet, are considered part of the evidence in determining whether remains will be repatriated or not. As I mentioned earlier, creation myths of the Umatilla were used in order to claim rights to the 9,300 year-old Kennewick Man skeleton.

In Hawaii, where groups have been extremely successful in reburials, religion is invoked many times. Edward Halealoha Ayau, executive director of Hui Malama I Na Kupuna O Hawaii Nei, writes in the 2007 article Rooted in Native Soil that Hui Malama of Hawaii "firmly believes that the repatriation and reburials were a direct result of intervention by God and the ancestors to inspire and energize us." Additionally, members of Hawaiian tribes are said to be inspired by spirits of the ancestors to take them home. Malama tribal members are against all scientific study and have been quoted as saying:

"We advocate against scientific study. In our view, such actions amounts to desecration-handling bones without prayer, without protocol, and with the intent to take without permission."

Furthermore, following my 2006 American Association for the Advancement of Science presentation and press release on how NAGPRA negatively affected scientific inquiry, I received many e-mail requests for more information. Some e-mail was reactionary; most individuals in favor of repatriation who contacted me seemed to have a spiritual investment. Much of the correspondence, for example, emphasized the importance of religion or spirituality over Western science. Martin D. Martinez III, the Chair of the Pomo Heritage Institute, for example, sent the following e-mail message entitled 'Sacred Sites stay sacred':

"I ask that you leave our Ancestors alone and let them do the Spiritual work they should focus on like saving some ones life from alcohol and drugs…Give some respect back to the Families and give back what was Native to the Native Families who should not have to go place to place and see their Ancestor's creations on display. It should be where it was laid to rest when they went home to Creator" [sic]

An e-mail from Kate Henderson again places the focus on religion:

"…you have no respect for our oral traditions, spirituality, or belief systems…We are ancient people whose belief systems are ingrained in our DNA, shame shame shame on you."

These e-mails and other correspondence have a sincerity that I do not doubt. The passion behind the convictions is true and the fervor is evident. These are all good religious qualities, but they fail under the tests of science, which is what repatriation and reburial laws should be based on. In fact, no government actions should be centered on religious convictions.

Others have highlighted the Native American perception of religious practices and reburial. San Francisco anthropologist Nani Ratnawati mentions a Native American who presented on NAGPRA at a national meeting; this individual stated that "the human remains of their ancestors are not 'dead bones' that can be probed and studied, but are the spirits of their ancestors that need to be buried properly." Also, at the American Anthropological Association conference, there have been many debates concerning the interwoven nature of reburial and religion. Dr. Ronald Grimes, a professor of religion at Wilfred Laurier University in Canada, has discussed religion's importance for Native Americans in the 2001 book *The Future of the Past*; he points out that one of the interesting aspects of the NAGPRA discussions were the continual declaration of the issue as essentially religious in nature by Native Americans themselves. Another example comes from Matthew King, who is the spiritual leader and chief of the Lakota Nation, when he stated that:

"After the immigrants came into our country, they started digging for graves, I don't know why…..They don't know God…..It [the land] is, a burial ground and also a church for our Indian people."

So, for anthropologists and other academics to claim that the issue of reburial is not a religious issue is a way of them denying the statements of tribal members. Even anthropologists who repeatedly provide evidence of the link between repatriation and religion often deny its association. Perhaps they think that accepting it as a religious issue will cause a loss of support among academics and other liberals; thus, they try to complicate the issue rather than respecting the Native American's claim of religion being the essential concern.

Interestingly, many Native Americans view the lack of burials as a reason for psychological and physical health problems as well as their social problems in the Native American communities. James Riding In wrote in the 2000 *Repatriation Reader: Who Owns American Indian Remains?*, for example, that "Wandering spirits often beset the living with psychological and health problems." Thus, anthropologists are at fault for a bevy of problems among Native Americans. The earlier email from Martin Martinez brings up this point as well ("let them [our ancestors] do the Spiritual work they should focus on like saving some ones life from alcohol and drugs").

Additionally, I received comments after the publication of my Society for American Archaeology newsletter article, such as from Dr. John Morris from the Alchimia Consultants that echo the religions sentiment of Native Americans. Dr. Morris states:

> "Her remark that many of her respondents seem to value human spirituality over Western science is surely true; there are far more people who value spirituality than who revere science to spirituality's exclusion, many of them noted scientists. These people's tax money supports our entire endeavor. She sees repatriation as "another religious attack on scientific inquiry," but does not seem to see that scientific analysis of human remains can also be viewed as another scientific attack on religion. It is crucial that all of us, from "both sides of the fence," work to reduce the current acrimony between popular religious feelings and scientific attitudes. Weiss's attitude would seem to be contributing more to the problem than to its solution."

Dr. Morris makes some extremely good points in his comments on my work. He has not misclassified me and I accept that most people do have religious beliefs (including many scientists). At the 2006 annual meeting of the American Association for the Advancement of Science, I was shocked to see how few scientists were willing to denounce religion. Where Morris is wrong is to assume that I do not see my view as an attack on religion by science. I am certainly taking an attack on religion; my dreams would follow those of John Lennon when he penned the lyrics to Imagine:

> Imagine there's no countries
>
> It isn't hard to do
>
> Nothing to kill or die for
>
> And no religion too
>
> Imagine all the people
>
> Living life in peace

What's more, I can imagine a world where there are no claims to the past and that the past belongs to everyone. Without creation stories, we could not claim that any of the tribes belong to any of the past populations without scientific evidence. Imagine if the tables were turned and we used our Christian creation story to explain our origins; would we not have to erase the millions of years of evolution, should we not claim any remains found in the Middle East? After all, Adam and Eve met a mere 6,000 years ago. If any of the human remains do not look like us, would that give us less of a claim on those skeletal individuals? I think that any academic would be in an uproar if Born-Again Christians tried to use their creation myth (of Adam and Eve) to repatriate and rebury Middle Eastern remains, such as Neanderthals!

SEPARATION OF CHURCH AND STATE: THE NAGPRA EXCEPTION

Another important point that arises from Morris's comment is the fact that tax money is used in all of these repatriation and reburial endeavors. I have no qualms about tax money being used to support scientific activities; the search for answers is in everyone's best interest. Can we really hold religion to the same rigorous level? Isn't there a separation of Church and State; so, tax money should not be used to support religious activities even if the tax payers are religious. Jerry Springer, an attorney in Illinois, has written a manuscript on just this aspect of repatriation and reburial laws. He clearly outlines how money from the government is used in repatriation and reburial, which are religious endeavors. When Native Americans claim ancestry through their creation myths and the US government takes those stories seriously enough to pay for repatriation and reburial, then the separation of Church and State has broken down.

In Jerry Springer's 2005-2006 article on Scholarship vs. Repatriationism in *Academic Questions* he covers the breakdown of Church and State separation and highlights the paradox between academics supporting repatriation, but not supporting other religious intrusions into federal institutions. He states that "repatriationism attempts to substitute animistic religion for history, anthropology, and the natural sciences." It seems that many academics as well accept and even support this substitution whereas I doubt they would support the substitution of science with Intelligent Design.

Church and State were separated in the First Amendment of the Constitution. The US Constitution states that "Congress shall make no law respecting an establishment of religion, or prohibiting the free exercise thereof." Federal courts have been very protective of the First Amendment in all cases that deal with religions, such as introducing creationism in schools, moments of silence enforced in federal institutions, and so forth. Still, NAGPRA has become the exception and animism is actually incorporated into the federal law! For this reason, the federal government is respecting a religious establishment when it supports various tribes and their religious leaders in claims on human remains. These are most definitely establishments of a religious nature.

The breakdown of Church and State separation is not just an implied point made by myself and others who are against repatriation and reburial. NAGPRA specifically requires consultation with religious leaders of tribes. NAGPRA states that federally funded institutions need to complete their inventories and the acts that follow "in consultation with tribal government and Native Hawaiian organization officials and traditional religious leaders." Another example is that review committees in NAGPRA will consist of at least two "traditional Indian religious leaders." Just recently, Interior Secretary Kempthorne appointed Donna Augustine, a Thunderbird Turtle Native American from Maine to one of NAGPRA's highest offices. Augustine, stated in a 2006 article in the *Native American Times*, is "recognized as a traditional religious leader by Indian tribes in the United States." This emphasis on religion is also present in CalNAGPRA as mentioned earlier and they carry on the tradition of requiring religious leaders in consultations.

Stephen Vincent, an investigative journalist who recently passed away, was a strong opponent of NAGPRA due to its religious overtones. In a 2004 article in *Reason Online*,

Stephen Vincent made it abundantly clear that NAGPRA is a religious law that destroys the separation of Church and State. He started his controversial article with:

> "Imagine an America where the federal government takes an active role in promoting the spiritual values of a certain cultural group. This group rarely documents its largely unknown religious practices and in fact considers many rituals too secret for public knowledge. Yet should outsiders violate its beliefs, the government can threaten them with lawsuits, fines, or prison sentences."

Then Vincent went on to highlight why this isn't imaginary. He stated that NAGPRA may have been ethically created to redress wrongs that were committed against the Native Americans. But, the law has encouraged the use of religious rationale to claim human remains and artifacts. The concept of sacred object and the emphasis on traditional folklore and creation myths has astounded critics of NAGPRA. Furthermore, the government pays for ceremonies and supports the various rituals and methods Native Americans claim for the treatment of these remains even though most Native Americans converted to Christianity and had previously sold "sacred objects." In 2006, NAGPRA has given out 2.4 million dollars in grants to Native American tribes and museums to assist in these religious endeavors. Some Native groups have been extremely successful in getting federal funding. Journalist Gordon Pang for the *Honolulu Advertiser*, for example, reported that the Hui Malama has received over a million dollars in less than 10 years, which the group claims has been mainly used for travel. Interestingly, the ability to get federal funding has led the group to become more aggressive in its reburials. Sometimes the aggressive reburial tactics employed are at the cost of other tribes that claim affiliation.

Most of these new "traditional" religions are not written down and they are also kept secret, making it possible for Native Americans to change traditions when they see fit. Anthropologists Drs. Michael Brown and Margaret Bruchac recently addressed the point of secrecy; they state "NAGPRA has itself contributed to Native anxiety over the movement of information because the law requires substantiating evidence to support repatriation claims." They, further, give the example of a Laguna Pueblo official named Paul Pino who put his concerns in to these words:

> "One of the things that really concerns me, is again, how much does the government have to know, and how much do the officials have to know with regards to the use and purpose, what these objects are for? Again, we're stuck in that position where disclosure means, you know, losing what safeguards we have with regards to those items."

Others too have addressed this matter of a lack of sharing knowledge with non-Natives. For example, Amy Dansie at the Nevada State Museum has told of her consultations with the Pauite and Shoshone in 1997 where she asked about the evidence concerning their oral history, including battles between groups and a lack of relatedness with other groups. The Native American tribes reacted by stating that these stories were lies told to white people and that Native Americans could not "share their sacred knowledge to explain why these stories, steadfastly maintained as fact" are no longer accepted as real. Could it be due to the fact that previously repatriation was not an issue? We must ask ourselves, why are the Native Americans so weary of disclosure when scientists are not? What do they have to hide and who do they not trust? And, can we trust them? Unfortunately, museum and NAGPRA officials are working on the issue of disclosure to comfort Native Americans rather than standing their ground and claiming that disclosure is necessary to show ancestry!

Dr. Kathleen Fine-Dare in her 2002 book writes of the importance of religion in the repatriation movement; her claim is that science and religion are basically equal and neither should be favored. She denies that there is a scientific truth and also denies that the Native Americans who demand reburial are fanatics. Nonetheless, she tells of how not reburying bones will bring bad fortune to those who work with the bones and have prevented Native Americans from progressing past poverty and addictions, as I mentioned others have also brought forth this claim.

I have provided ample evidence of the importance of religion to Native Americans in repatriation and reburial deeds. Academics who deny the religious importance to these individuals are showing a lack of sensitivity to those they claim to support or maybe even a lack of trust in the Native Americans. Given that repatriation is about religion, let us consider a similar scenario arising in biology. What if biologists were required to consult with religious leaders over evolutionary evidence? This would be equivalent to science teachers being required to teach creationism or Intelligent Design in public classrooms; a proposition I suspect nearly all academics are strongly against. Yet, many of them continue to support the efforts of Native American tribes repatriating and reburying remains on the basis of their creation stories. Ironically, support comes from academics and liberals biggest enemies as well.

SUPPORT FROM THE RELIGIOUS RIGHT

The repatriation and reburial movement has received much support from the religious right. Christian fundamentalists are pleased to inhibit explanations of human origins via evolution and prevent the destruction of their own creation myth. Scientists strongly oppose the religious right; I have never met an academic in favor of upholding the creation myths of Christianity or teach the new myth of Intelligent Design. When the religious right uses their creation stories to explain the world; Western academia is up in arms. So, why then do we support the creation myths of others? So, why can we not see that the religious right has been backing NAGPRA as a way of fighting the true story of the peopling of the Americas? By not studying bones and accepting creation myths, the religious right does not need to explain why the Bible says the earth is only 6,000 years old, but we have skeletons of modern humans dating to nearly 10,000 years in North America! When we help Native Americans rebury their remains, we help the religious right avoid dealing with issues that negate their own agendas. Fundamentalists never seek the truth; rather, they try to hide facts and base their religion (as do all religions) on faith. I ask them then to take a big leap of faith and face the scientific evidence; can their religion hold up to scientific rigor?

Scientists constantly question their own hypotheses because we know in the end that the truth is more important than any one idea. With the religious right helping NAGPRA and academics on the same side as the religious right, we must ask ourselves does this leak into other parts of our world, such as into the classrooms and the debate about including religious hypotheses in science classes.

HUMAN RIGHTS ISSUE

Some people have argued that the classification of NAGPRA as a religious versus science debate is false; rather they point to evidence that NAGPRA was passed as a human rights legislation. Dr. David Hurst Thomas, who is currently the curator of anthropology at the American Museum of Natural History, has said that NAGPRA is an important human rights act that allows living Native Americans to practice their traditional religious responsibilities towards the dead. Human rights in the US consist of the Bill of Rights (which includes the First Amendment to the constitution that states "Congress shall make no law respecting an establishment of religion, or prohibiting the free exercise thereof."). Furthermore, the UN declaration of human rights also supports freedom of religion in Article 18. Thus, supporters of NAGPRA state that the law enables Native Americans to freely practice their religion. Their traditional religions, they claim include respect for their deceased and creation myths that tell them that they were here from the beginning of time.

Some of the human rights movement in Native American societies was due to the lack of rights over the last two centuries; and, some Native Americans, such as Armand Minthorn (of the Umatilla tribe), felt that NAGPRA has redressed some wrongs. However, he and others still have complaints that the funding isn't sufficient and that progress isn't fast enough. Moreover, none of the tribes seem to be overly concerned with actual relatedness of skeletal remains, even though in some tribes burying the enemies of others is against the traditional ways. Some of the traditional religion is not supported by evidence, for example, in Hawaii many tribes seem to make up practices as they go along and there is nothing supporting that these are long-standing practices. Therefore, it seems that true traditional ways are not necessarily being followed and the act of scientific knowledge has taken the backseat to religion perhaps as a power play disguised as human rights.

One must also ask whether human rights regarding religion should be supported through tax-payers monies. After all, couldn't Christian Creationists argue that in order to practice their religion children should learn about Intelligent Design in schools? And, do Rastafarians get a free pass to smoke pot for their religion? Not all religious practices are legal and people are prosecuted for their "religious" actions when they are not legal. A prominent example comes from Mormons who claim that having more than one wife is a religious freedom that they should be allowed to engage in, although these are the minority of Mormons. Will Muslims be allowed to have more than one wife in the US due to human rights laws?

Human rights do enable religious freedom (which includes the right not to be religious), but in the UN declaration of human rights it also includes the protection of science. In article 27, the declaration states: "Everyone has the right freely to participate in the cultural life of the community, to enjoy the arts and to share in scientific advancement and its benefits." By destroying the science of bioarchaeology through reburial, we cannot all share in scientific advancement and the benefits it will provide. One of those benefits includes knowledge of the past, freedom from superstition, and a broadening of the mind through an understanding of the past rather than just a focus on the present. The second part of article 27 states: "Everyone has the right to the protection of the moral and material interests resulting from any scientific, literary or artistic production of which he is the author." This basically can be understood as scientists have a right to protect their materials, whether that includes writings or data (such as human remains). NAGPRA destroys this protection and thereby conflicts with the human rights of scientists.

MORE THAN ONE TRUTH

Some other people who address repatriation and reburial issues claim that it is not a question of science versus religion; they argue that the Native American's way of understanding the past is merely another way to understand the past. There is not only one past, they state. Furthermore, they take umbrage at giving more weight to the scientific reconstructions of the past rather than buying into the narrative stories and traditional lore of Native Americans. It has been argued by many that science isn't the only way of knowing the past. There has been a movement by liberal academics to accept more than one type of knowledge. Those who support NAGPRA and other state laws concerning repatriation and reburial are at the forefront of this movement. Different epistemologies (which can be defined as different worldviews) are thought to be equally valid by these individuals; however, this ignores that there isn't more than one past. How can more than one way of explaining the past be accepted when the past only occurred one time? How can the oral traditions and the scientific evidence that directly contradict each other both have validity?

Archaeologists are not in agreement with each reconstruction and sometimes there are heated debates over topics, such as the peopling of the Americas, spread of diseases, the affect of agriculture on populations, and many other things. In science, conversely, we all value debates and recognize that hypotheses can be tested and different stories about the past can be told with the same data, but that new data can also create cause for reconstructing past stories. The difference between this and accepting the religious mythology is that religion doesn't allow for debate; the Native American creation stories do not rely on new data analysis and do not allow for challenges to that reconstruction. There are many ways to understand the past, but they are all driven by science. Otherwise, why don't we hold evolutionary past and creationism to the same assessment? Couldn't we claim that there is more than one way to understand all of the past and, thus, we should give religions of all sorts the same weight as science?

The fact as I mentioned earlier is that there isn't more than one past; there is only a lack of complete knowledge about the past as there always will be. Science, however, is the only way to accurately reconstruct the past and will be the only method to provide us with real answers. Furthermore, science is the only field that allows for a challenge of their reconstructions.

If repatriation and reburial isn't about religion, then why do Native Americans not want the remains to be examined? Why are they afraid of challenges to their stories of the past? Shouldn't the most accurate story be the one told rather than the most politically correct, sensitive, or ethical story?

One of my favorite quotes comes from Dr. Ian Tattersall, the current curator at the American Museum of Natural History, in a film done on human evolution; he defines religion and science as: "science is a system based on doubt, whereas religion is a system based on faith." Thus, although many people may be religious; the fact is that science is the only system of learning based on asking questions and being able to refute answers and revise knowledge. It becomes the only way to know what really happened. This is not to say that scientific knowledge is free of personal biases or that politics never takes place in science; however, science can be repeated and corrected whereas religious stories do not have that methodology in place. So, if a scientist has let his own views color his finding, others will test his 'truths' in order to determine whether they are accurate. Moreover, if they are inaccurate, they will be replaced with the newer, more accurate reconstructions. This occurs repeatedly in science and is the reason for the strength of science as a way of understanding the world around us.

Native oral histories are not valid by themselves; they are only valid tested through the scientific method and supported by evidence. Saying something is so, shouldn't be enough to ruin a scientific field of inquiry. When people accuse me of having the view that biological evidence should outweigh other types of evidence; they are correct in their assessment. I do think that burying evidence is a way to prop up myths and that these myths are not another way of gaining knowledge, but rather a way to prevent knowledge from being gained. I am not alone in this view. Dr. Douglas Owsley, who is one of the anthropologists who fought for the right to study Kennewick Man, has stated that "a clear and accurate understanding of the ancient past is something that the American public has a right to know about" in Mysteries of the First Americans (a NOVA program that appeared in 2000). Additionally, anthropologist Jim Chatters, the first anthropologist who looked at Kennewick Man, has been quoted as saying "Just don't talk about the truth. It might offend somebody" in a 1998 edition of the *Nevada Journal* with regards to the repatriation of another ancient human remains that does not appear to be related to modern Native Americans. Anthropologists and other scientists should be aghast at the governments siding with Indian mythology over scientific evidence. Dr. G. A. Clark, at the Arizona State University, has published a strong letter in support of one way of understanding the past; the scientific way. In the Society for American *Archaeology Bulletin*, Clark states that:

> "it seems that the worldview of Western science is under serious and sustained assault…a multipronged attack in which mysticism, religious fundamentalism, creationism and belief in the paranormal…attack the critical realism and mitigated objectivity that are the central epistemological biases of the scientific worldview."

Amy Dansie of the Nevada State Museum has also supported scientific evidence over the religious mythologies. She stated her interactions with Native peoples has made her realize that those with traditional understandings of the universe do not agree with physical facts, genetics, historic continuity, or any other realities that interfere with their view of the creator and religious opinions. Interestingly, she is able to see the different viewpoints and yet hold on to the value of the scientific view over other stories. In 1999, she wrote quite clearly over the tension surrounding the study of early Paleo-Indians and modern Native Americans and stated that she values "scientific knowledge about their past more than their own religious beliefs" and she was "not yet ready to abandon this virtually hopeless battle" of religion versus science in the field of prehistoric America.

What I find most troublesome is that this attack is being supported by academics. By arguing that there is more than one way of understanding the world, we open up the door to all crackpot ideas; including those such as the Native American creation myths. Scientific evidence has found support repeatedly for the travel of peoples from the Asian regions to the Americas (one of those travels occurred across the Bering Land Bridge, but others came before and after). Scientists have redrawn their reconstructions to encompass new evidence and have made progress in understanding the peopling of the Americas. But, Native Americans repeatedly deny this evidence; Armand Minthorn (who was appointed by President Clinton to serve on NAGPRA's review committee) has been quoted in the Nevada Journal as saying "We didn't come across no land bridge. We have always been here." Dr. Larry Zimmerman, an archaeologist at the Purdue University in Indiana, has gone native and supports the mythologies of the Native Americans with statements on how anthropologists need to understand how Native Americans view the past and how there is more than one past. And, thus, in turn more than one type of knowledge. More sensible anthropologists support the use of science in favor of the use of tradition. Dr. Clark, for example, has been quoted as saying Indians "haven't always been where they are found today, regardless of what their origins myths might say." Dr. Reinhard has also been a staunch supporter of seeing the world through scientific lenses. I side myself with these anthropologists who see reality and myths as separate rather than just different perspectives.

Chapter 8

REPATRIATION AND REBURIAL EFFECTS ON SCIENTIFIC INQUIRY

"Does NAGRPA and the ongoing process of repatriation and reburial ring the death knell for bioarchaeology as a research paradigm and profession?"

> *Jerome C. Rose et al. (1996: NAGPRA is Forever:*
> *Osteology and the repatriation of skeletons.*
> *Annual Review of Anthropology Vol. 25).*

PREDICTIONS VERSUS OUTCOMES ON HOW NAGPRA HAS AFFECTED SCIENCE

I am willing to admit that my bias against NAGPRA and other repatriation and reburial laws set in early in my career. Prior to studying Native American remains, I had feared that all the paleoanthropological fossils would be uncovered before I ever finished graduate school. While that particular fear was definitely ungrounded (as we witness new fossils being discovered every year), it highlights my state of mind concerning scientific endeavors. Throughout my graduate career, I heard of remains being reburied. Then, while I was collecting the data for my Ph.D. dissertation at the Canadian Museum of Civilization in Ottawa the reburial of the museum's largest skeletal collection was underway. The Haida Native Americans were claiming 151 skeletal individuals. Mark MacKinnon, a reporter for Canada's *Globe and Mail* newspaper, began his August 2000 article as follows:

> "After spending an entire century in the basement of a museum in Ottawa being probed and prodded by scientists, the remains of two Haida men and one Haida woman are finally on the way to British Columbia, where they will be buried for a second time near the ocean where the three spent their days. The three skulls and jawbones were among 148 sets of skeletal remains returned to the Haida."

The Haida wanted more than just the skeletal remains. During the repatriation, the Haida walked the corridors of the museum's research facility beating their drums to appease the spirits. Museum workers and officials participated in Native American rituals on the museum grounds for the spirits of the skeletons and attended a "Feast to Show Respect." Another request of the Haida (which was being negotiated at the time) was for the destruction of the casts made of some of the bones. No scientist will be able to study this large collection again. This horrifying experience added to my already strong feelings against repatriation.

I saw letters that suggested that the sample I was working with was also in threat of repatriation. I had X-rayed the bones of over 100 individuals from the Tsimshin tribe of the British Columbia coast dating between 3,500 to 1,500 BP (before present). Although the Haida have no affiliation with these Tsimshin remains, museum officials feared the Haida would object to seeing other Native American bones being studied and I was required to keep a low profile. Subsequently, probably based on the lists of the remains that the museum is required to publish for Native activists, the sample I worked on has attracted attention and has probably disappeared forever.

Not all anthropologists have the same concerns that I do. Some anthropologists think that repatriation and reburial is good for the ethics of the science and perhaps even the research aspect of anthropology. Most anthropologists take a moderate position. They are not opposed to reburying "affiliated remains," those that can be shown to have a cultural or geographical link to a modern Native population. For example, the American Association of Physical Anthropologists has an official position that is generally sympathetic to repatriation, which they have posted on their website (http://www.physanth.org) when there is cultural affiliation present. What constitutes evidence for this affiliation is not out-lined. In principle at least, the American Association of Physical Anthropologists is opposed to the reburial of non-affiliated remains (such as Kennewick Man):

> "The American Association of Physical Anthropologists supports the rights of Native Americans to claim human remains and funerary objects in cases where the modern group is culturally affiliated with the remains in question…Where cultural affiliation exists, repatriation claims must be honored; but where cultural affiliation is absent, repatriation claims have no moral foundation."

Anthropologists Michael Brown and Margaret Bruchac recently wrote in general anthropologists "support NAGRPA, but remain uneasy about its implications for future anthropological research." I would agree with this statement. Anthropologists see repatriation and reburial as righting wrongs that have been inflicted on Native Americans (and other minority groups). They often are guilt ridden as a result of decades of blaming present anthropologists on supposed sins of our anthropological forefathers without consideration of the different ethos of the times or even just that modern anthropologists have no control of the past. Should Native Americans start to feel guilty for taking body parts as trophies in their past wars? We have strong evidence from California and the Southwest that prehistoric population tool arms, legs, hands, and feet of their enemies that they had slain during times of conflict.

Other anthropologists have argued that repatriation would be good for science. In 1996, Jerome Rose at the University of Arkansas and some of his colleagues, for example, put forth the theory that repatriation would eliminate gaps in knowledge of specific times and geographical regions, require osteological analyses to be more comprehensive than before, increase the use of new methodologies, improve curation facilities, and finally create a more ethical discipline. I disagree with these stated opinions. And, since the onset of my career held the opinion that reburial of any remains detracts from the ability of anthropologists to understand humankind scientifically. However, since I am trained as a scientist, I decided to conduct a study to determine whether my worries about the loss of skeletal remains and, therefore, the demise of North American bioarchaeology were imaginary or real.

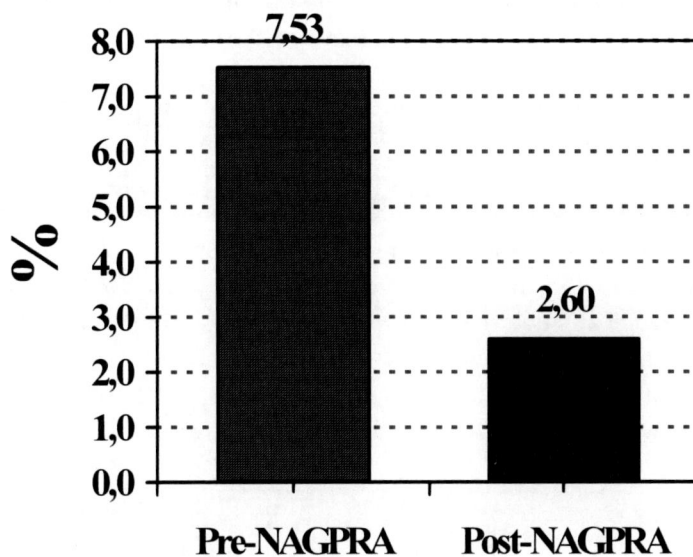

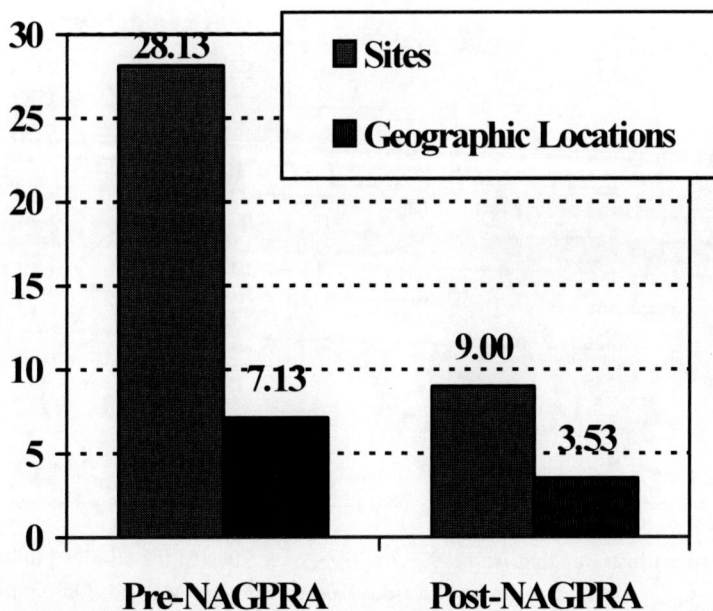

Figures 15. Top (a) shows the decline in percentage of osteological studies using Native American remains. Bottom (b) shows the decline in number of sites and geographic variance. All of these changes are statistically significant. Both data sets were initially presented at 2006 annual meeting of the American Association for the Advancement of Science.

In order to determine the true effects of NAGPRA on research, I examined 30 years of *American Journal of Physical Anthropology* issues. This is the top journal of the field and a good indicator of the direction in which the field is going in. I chose to look at the past 30 years since I looked at 15 years prior to the passing of NAGPRA and 15 years after the passing of NAGPRA. I took the predictions that I mentioned earlier from Dr. Rose and his colleagues and examined the shifts in the literature. Basically, I wanted to see if after NAGPRA was passed there would be a greater number of studies varying in time periods, geographies, and more comprehensive analyses. What my results showed was that any shifts that were visible or statistically significant were in the direction opposite to those predicted by previous anthropologists. Compared to pre-NAGPRA, osteological studies containing Native American remains went down, fewer different sites were used and less geographic locations were examined (Figures 15a, b). Both before and after NAGPRA was enacted, over 70 percent of the osteological studies come from sites in nine states and research using Native American human remains significantly decreased in four (Alaska, Arizona, Kentucky, and Ohio) out of the nine states (Figure 16). NAGPRA, my own research has shown, has negatively affected scientific studies.

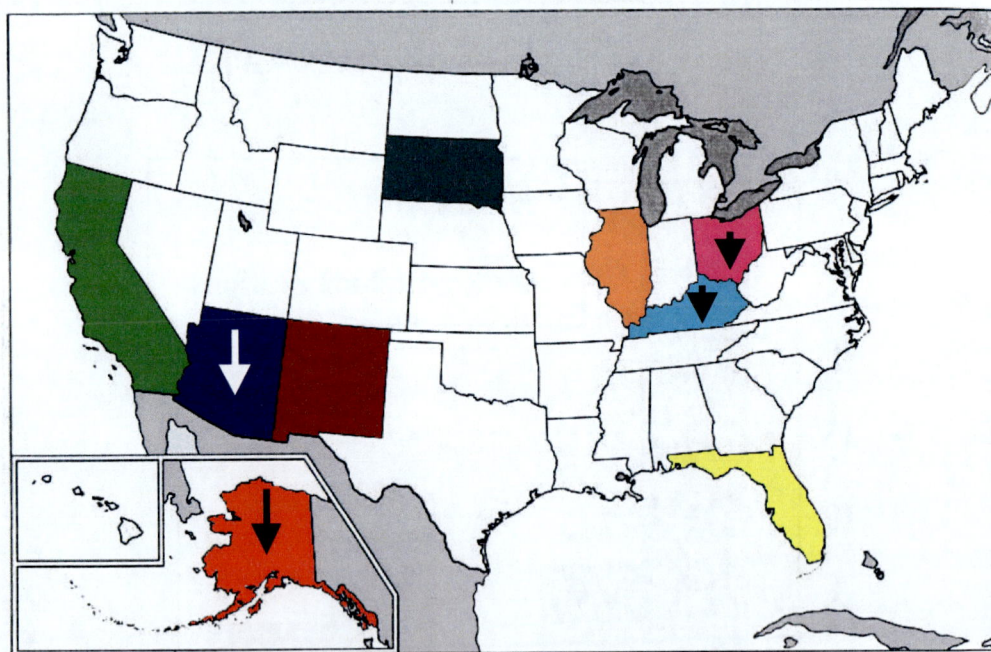

Figure 16. This figure illustrates that from 1975 to 2005, over 70% of the studies published use remains from 9 states (Alaska, Arizona, California, Florida, Kentucky, New Mexico, Ohio, and South Dakota). Arrows show statistically significant decreases in osteological research in four out of nine of the states from Pre-NAGPRA to Post-NAGPRA.

Not everyone agrees with my conclusions. In regards to the above research, I was interviewed by Sam Lewin, a journalist for *the Native American Times*, in 2006 via telephone to try to get a more complete picture of the issue. Lewis wrote an excellent article that was balanced and well researched. In this article, Sherry Hutt of the Smithsonian Repatriation Committee stated that NAGPRA has not impeded research, but has enhanced it. This, nonetheless, is not reflected in anthropological publication of research. Furthermore, she stated, "many of the human remains in collections were not collected using scientific methods and therefore repatriation of those remains would have little or no bearing on science." I would have to disagree, even if the sample was not ideally collected, we can still learn a lot about bone biology, health, and the past in general from good sample sizes. Only more research on the topic can resolve this disagreement, which is why I have attempted to do a more thorough review of the osteological work being conducted by looking at the outcome of dissertations and theses, which are final research projects that are on the topics soon to be the graduates focus in their careers, from anthropology departments in the US using the same criteria.

What I found was a similar trend in graduate theses and dissertations. Before the enactment of NAGPRA, skeletal studies on Native American bones constituted about 12% of theses and dissertation; whereas, for the same length of time (15 years), there is a drastic increase in dissertations regarding skeletal remains and anthropology (from about 9 to over 300), but the percentage of those that involve Native American remains drops to around 5%. This is a statistically significant decrease. Furthermore, NAGRPA didn't create more diversity in data sources; the same sites and states were repeatedly used (probably because of availability and sample size). In consequence, NAGPRA has even hit graduate student research. What this implies is that fewer students are going to explore and become experts in bioarchaeology. It is the front end of a trend that indicates a decline in American osteology. Fewer graduates, fewer researchers, and fewer professors to reveal the true prehistory of the Americas. This decrease may be due to a waning in students' interest, but this is not likely since other areas of osteology have stayed robust. It seems that this decrease is due to a greater difficulty in accessing remains, a negative aura in the field of studying Native American remains, and, perhaps, advisors telling students to conduct safer research.

LOSS OF DATA AND FUNDING

When your research is centered on the study of human remains, removing those remains from availability has to be seen as a loss of data. Since NAGPRA has been enacted no one knows for sure how many remains have been repatriated or reburied. The federally funded institutions are not required to keep this information and neither is the federal government. They do publish a list per year of number of requests for repatriation and the numbers are frightening. In 2006, 360 notices of intent to repatriate were published, which accounts for 118,442 funerary objects, 3,585 sacred objects, 296 objects of cultural patrimony, and 768 sacred objects that are also cultural patrimony. In the fiscal year of 2006, 2,370 human remains were returned upon discovery and an additional 2,175 remains have been identified for repatriation!

What we do know about the overall loss of remains comes from newspaper and Internet articles. The numbers are not always in accord with each other, but they are in ballpark ranges of each other. For example, according to an Associated Press article published in 2004, more than 27,000 individuals have been repatriated since the passage of NAGPRA. Tom Paulson, the science writer for the *Seattle Post*, found that by 2000, about 14,000 human remains have been repatriated. In March 2006, the *New York Times* ran an article by Edward Rothstein that suggests even higher numbers. Rothstein states that "according to federal statistics by 2005, remains of more than 30,000 individuals" had been repatriated. An article by Jim Erickson about Pueblo reburials in the *Rocky Mountain News*, states that by 2006, 32,052 individuals have been repatriated through NAGPRA. Additionally, over half a million funerary objects have been returned to tribes.

Some of the large repatriations that have occurred include over 1500 Ancient Pueblo Indians, which included 455 nearly complete skeletons according to Jim Erickson of the *Rocky Mountain News* in a May 2006 article. The University of Pennsylvania's museum (Penn Museum) has had many repatriations over the last 15 years; their largest included repatriating 120 remains to the Chugach Alaskans. The Maxwell Museum of Anthropology at University of New Mexico has also had several repatriations and allows no photography of currently curated prehistoric remains (although you can take pictures of their non-Native remains). In May 1999, nearly 2000 human remains were reburied at Pecos National Historical Park; this collection had been a vast resource for anthropologists for decades and was housed at the Peabody Museum of Archaeology and Ethnology in Massachusetts. There are 4000 human remains that have been repatriated from Kentucky's universities according to anthropologist Dr. James Baird. The Native American Rights Fund has proudly represented the Pawnee Nation with their repatriation claim of 800 human remains in Nebraska; these remains have now been reburied.

The Smithsonian Institute, possibly holding the largest collection of prehistoric skeletal individuals, has been losing a steady stream of their collections since the onset of repatriation laws. They have repatriated 3,591 skeletal individuals out of the 5,000 sets of human remains that fall under federal repatriation laws. The Smithsonian's Museum of Natural History has returned a large portion of its 18,500 human remains.

The Umatilla, the same tribe who fought to rebury 9,300 year-old Kennewick Man, repatriated 240 individuals in 2006. In Hawaii, repatriation and reburial is a very hot topic and in January 2006, Gordon Pang wrote in the *Honolulu Advertiser* that 2,900 sets of remains had been reburied and another 3,000 have been repatriated. Just this year, 131 individuals were repatriated from the Washington Museum in Washington State. This was the largest repatriation in the Northwest. Human remains from the San Diego Museum of Man and the Burke Museum in Seattle were reburied in February 2007 by the Confederated Tribes of the Umatilla Indian Reservation. And, also this year, another 143 individuals, who had been rescued from destruction during the construction of the Ice Harbor Dam over 40 years ago, were repatriated from Washington State. The Umatillas have contacted over 130 museums and other federally funded institutes in order to repatriate as many human remains as possible (even if the remains have only the slightest bit of connection to their past).

Even prior to NAGPRA, in 1989, Stanford University anticipating NAGPRA enactment repatriated 550 human remains to the Ohlone-Costanoan tribe, which is the same tribe that claims affiliation to the remains housed at San Jose State University. Actually, these Stanford University remains were housed at San Jose State University prior to repatriation. Stanford University's actions under NAGPRA would be considered illegal now since the Ohlone-Costanoans are not even federally recognized! As a result, we lost more than 2/3 of a population for no reason. Even now, institutions are trying to be at the forefront of political correctness by being proactive in returning remains. In a 2006 article in LJWorld.com by Sophia Maines, a Kansas University lecturer Bobbi Rahdar states, "The university would like to be proactive in repatriating the remains." Plus, finally, Haida Canadian Indians have repatriated human remains from Oakland Museum in California and the American Museum of Natural History in New York. Chicago's Field Museum returned the bones of 150 people to the Haida tribe in British Columbia. They are militaristic about repatriation and have so far reburied over 200 individuals from Canadian collections and over 187 individuals and counting from US collections.

In his 1999 book *The New Know-Nothings*, Morton Hunt reported on the extent on some of the more controversial repatriations of Indian bones. He found that the Buhl Burial, the skeleton of a woman more than 10,000 years old found in Idaho together with grave goods – one of the oldest remains yet found in North America, and valuable evidence of the origins of the peopling of the continent – has been repatriated by the Shoshone-Bannock tribe and reburied without being adequately studied. Another of the earliest specimens, the nearly 8,000-year-old Hourglass Cave skeleton from the Colorado Rockies, has been reclaimed and reburied by the Southern Utes. Another early specimen is the Browns Valley man who was found in Minnesota; he was dated to nearly 9,000 years old and in moderate condition. No evidence was found to link the Browns Valley male to modern Native Americans; yet, he was reburied by the Sioux Indians of South Dakota in 1999. Another specimen was buried at the same time as Browns Valley man; Pelican Rapids woman, a nearly 8,000-year-old teen-age female, also from Minnesota and also showing no affinity to the modern Native Americans. Prospect Man from Oregon is a slightly more modern Paleo-Indian dated to 6,800 years-old who has been repatriated although the similarity to modern American Indians was slight and no DNA testing was ever completed. Another very early specimen, a 9,400-year-old mummy from Spirit Cave in Nevada has been claimed, though not yet reburied, by the Northern Pauite. Spirit Cave is still in legal limbo and has not been available to scientists for study. As pointed out on the Friends of America's Past website, Spirit Cave is almost 500 human generations removed from modern peoples; "this is twice the age of the Egyptian pyramids and more than four times the age of the Mayan pyramids in Central America." Others in legal limbo include, Wizards Beach Man a 9,200 year-old Nevada specimen; Grimes Point Burial also from Nevada and around 9,000 years old; an 18 month old child from Montana dated at nearly 11,000 years old and the only human remains associated with Clovis (which is perhaps the first stone tool culture in the Americas) artifacts. And, finally the 9,700 year-old female from Gordon Creek Colorado is also in peril. Paleo-Indians are of particular concern because there are so few of them and each one is precious in order to be able to gain a better understanding of the earliest Americans. Because these remains are not very likely to be related to modern groups, by repatriating them a can of worms is opened up to allow the reburial of all non-European remains in the Americas.

Morton Hunt also reported on some culturally unaffiliated remains being reburied. For example, unidentifiable remains of 821 individuals from the University of Nebraska have been repatriated. Over a thousand culturally unaffiliated remains have been repatriated to the Sioux tribes of the Dakotas. Additionally, the Hopi tribe in Arizona has demanded a complete moratorium on access by researchers to field notes, photographs, sound and video recording, and other archival materials about their tribes held at museums, research libraries, and universities. On the National Park Service website, they also list in their culturally unidentifiable section that

> "Among the human remains included there are 5,238 that have been affiliated or transferred since they were first inventoried as culturally unidentifiable."

Not surprisingly, some anthropologists and archaeologists are aghast at the prospect of the permanent loss of access to so much knowledge. Anthropologists, like Mike O'Brien at Missouri University, have said that returning bones is like burning books. Amy Dansie and Donald Tuohy of the Nevada State Museum wrote in the 1997 issue of the Anthropology Newsletter "despite the general assumption that science is free to inquire where it will, science is no longer free in the realm of human prehistory." The loss of data has not stopped and each year thousands of remains discovered through excavation (mostly due to construction) are returned to Native Americans almost immediately, which stops the progress of scientific study of newly discovered remains.

The NAGPRA process is a slow one, which is often lamented by Native American tribes; thus, many collections have yet to be repatriated or reburied. This does not mean, however, that the skeletal remains are available to science. Even when the remains have yet to be reburied, they may be lost for study. Sacramento State University, where I had done my Master's work, has discontinued allowing students and other researchers access to the skeletal collection housed in their facilities. Their Master's students travel as far as England to gain access to remains to study when there is a large skeletal collection housed right in their building! What this means is that students are losing the opportunity to study a collection at all; costs of travel may reduce the likelihood of completion of their thesis. Also, the time that they complete their studies may be increased greatly; making a Master's into as long a process as a Ph.D.

Collections from previous times are not the only thing being buried. Each year when individuals are found, reburials occur. Many times these new reburials occur quickly and quietly. With Native Americans in the field, there is little doubt who will lay claim to these individuals and that they will be reburied. Currently, at my own university, there is continual collaboration with the Muwekma-Ohlone who run an archaeological consulting firm as well. These Native Americans lack the federal recognition required to rebury bones under NAGPRA, but they proceed with reburials any time skeletal remains are discovered, such as when skeletal remains were discovered while doing conducting fieldwork for the expansion of Stanford University's athletic grounds. Although many of the remains found may seem of little interest, are not well preserved, or lack large numbers, without new samples while our old samples are being removed from access, the field will change into an application driven field rather than a scientific one. In other words, anthropologists will no longer be able to ask and research questions regarding the past. Instead, we will be used to answer questions mandated by reburial and repatriation laws, such as sex, age, and affiliation.

Not only has data been lost, but funding as well has been lost. There has been a great deal of money that has gone into the implementation of NAGRPA, but at the cost of real research. In 2006, Brown and Bruchac pointed out that it is impossible to actually calculate the impact of NAGPRA on museums and other institutions since money going into these institutions is being used to hire individuals to help with inventories and repatriations, rather than research. Also, time is of issue; anthropologists have had to curtail their research in order to aid in repatriation rather than answer the scientific questions they ask in their minds in order to truly understand the past better. For example, Amy Dansie at the Nevada State Museum, has stated in her 1999 paper in the Society for American Archaeology Bulletin that the efforts of following NAGPRA has "resulted in 10,000 hours spent over the past nine years of my life" and NAGPRA work is on-going "sucking day after day, year after year, out of our careers."

These lost hours are spent on inventory, consultations, studying the law, and trying to figure out NAGPRA in a sincere effort to be in compliance.

Furthermore, some journalists have pointed out that the true affect on institutions has not been properly assessed. George Johnson, a writer for the *New York Times*, has been quoted as saying, "Privately, some say they are afraid that if they take too strong a stand in favor of scientific inquiry, they will be denied more research opportunities." Anthropologists are often tempered in their discussions of NAGPRA and are scared to speak up against NAGPRA excesses. Anthropologists have told me of repatriation and reburial horrors, how they thought that NAGPRA was hurting science, and how scientific inquiry is being deterred through repatriation; yet, nearly none of these scientists is willing to write letters against NAGPRA or speak openly about these issues. NAGPRA has created an aura of fear in academia that is not present in the other sciences. Universities, as well, are not willing to step up against NAGPRA abuses; for example, the universities of the scientists who fought against the reburial of Kennewick Man provided no financial or moral support to these brave individuals. Anthropologist Richard Jantz from the University of Tennessee has been quoted in the *Nevada Journal* by writer Dowd Muska as saying: "Our institutions are typically mainly concerned with keeping themselves out of controversy." And, even the anthropological and scientific national organizations are reluctant to take a strong stand against NAGPRA abuses.

STANDARDIZATION AND SCIENCE

Science works through replication; what this means is that we should be able to find the same results with new studies that are conducted in the same manner. Data across studies should be comparable so that we can look at different populations in the same manner and notice trends and differences to enable us to understand the past. When you have a science where data is being reburied like in bioarchaeology, standardization is crucial. By not standardizing the data, we lose the ability to compare populations that have already been studied, but are now reburied or repatriated. Some anthropologists have lauded NAGPRA for creating the need for standardization in a generally un-standardized field. For example, in 1993 Drs. Anthony Klesert and Shirley Powell of Northern Arizona University pointed out that NAGPRA would result in a more uniform set of standards for the study of human subjects. The 1994 book by anthropologists Dr. Jane Buikstra and Douglas Ubelaker *Standards: For Data Collection from Human Skeletal Remains* was published in part as a reaction to the passing of NAGPRA and provides uniform procedures for examining skeletons. In my 2006 study on the affect of NAGPRA on science, I looked at whether the Standards was used in published studies. What I found was appalling; only about a third of the osteological studies published after 1994 use *Standards: For Data Collection from Human Skeletal Remains*. These same dismal numbers were also found in dissertations and theses. What this means is that NAGPRA has not created a way to collect data in a standard method that scientists readily employ and our studies are not comparable without having the remains to collect data anew. In the past, anthropologists would just recollect the data in their way for comparisons, but with the loss of data this isn't possible. As a consequence, we will have a hodge-podge of data and the lack of comparability will greatly reduce validity of answering questions that cross time periods and cultures.

LOSS OF SCIENTIFIC FREEDOM

One of the scariest aspects of repatriation and reburial to me is the loss of scientific freedom. Scientists should be able to attempt to answer all sorts of questions about the world around them, which includes the past. These questions should not be hampered by political or religious sentiments. Furthermore, these questions shouldn't be determined by laws that favor religion over science. Laws, such as NAGPRA and CalNAGPRA, shape the type of questions that will be asked and answered by researchers. In fact, the ideology surrounding reburial threatens freedom of scientific inquiry. Once bones have been returned, they can no longer be studied without the permission of the Amerindian tribes who hold the rights to the bones, which is rarely forthcoming, especially after they have been reburied. This means that when new technologies arise, the material is no longer available.

Since the passing of NAGRPA, affiliation research become of key importance, although real scientific evidence of affiliation is often not required to repatriate bones. Also, repatriation laws are written as to severely inhibit anthropologists' time limits on studies. When bones are in danger of repatriation, large studies that contain large samples and answer important questions, such as shifts in health with changes in subsistence patterns and climatic shift effects on the health of populations, cannot be conducted. With repatriation in the picture, anthropologists may be scared to start large studies. After all, what if they start a study and 5 years into it the bones become slotted for repatriation? Projects that may require years to complete will be out of the question. Some questions that may require more time include analyses of whole populations, such as demographic studies to determine leading causes of death in a population. Other studies that require many measurements, such as osteological analyses of skulls to draw family trees, may also require more than a year for large samples. Studies that require technical assistance, such as X-rays, CT-scans, MRIs, and DNA analyses, often require more than a year since obtaining access to equipment is often done through medical facilities that slip anthropologists' work in when patients are few.

The laws allow for completion of studies that have been started, but on the contingency that they "would be of major benefit to the United States. Such items shall be returned by no later than 90 days after the date on which the scientific study is completed." Who will be determining whether the study is a major benefit to the United States? If Native Americans on the review committee are part of that process, we can be sure that beneficial standings are rarely meted out. What if a study is a major benefit to the field of anthropology and, therefore, the American public who deserve to know more about the past, but a setback for Native Americans or religion? Are anthropologists, then, bound to just answer questions that will be quickly completed or use smaller samples to answer questions that could be answered better with larger samples. Time is always important and often times scientific studies can take years, new techniques sometimes arise, or problems come up that make starting anew essential. Just imagine how awful it must be if you are scared to start a study because it may take longer than 30 days!

The other aspect of this time limit is that only the scientists who have immediate access to the remains will be likely to study them. Scientists from other institutions are unlikely to meet the time limits when they may have to schedule flights or work around teaching schedules. Should only those at the institutions where the remains are housed be able to conduct research? This has never been the case in anthropology where we feel strongly that the past belongs to everyone and that housing skeletal remains does not mean owning them.

Another loss of scientific freedom is encountered when tribal consultation or supervision is required. Tribes are not likely to allow the study of remains if the questions may be controversial or conflict with their creation myths. Should a biologist be required to ask a religious leader about the study of evolution? What if an anthropologist seeks to answer questions about when certain groups made the journey to the Americas and yet the Native Americans say, "Heck, we never made the trip our creation story tells us we have always been here?" This is a ridiculous situation to be in. Anthropologists have studied in order to be objective scientists and learn the true prehistory of the locations they are examining; the loss of freedom to answer these questions is an affront on our training and our ethics. Many Native Americans have strong anti-science feelings as stated in this quote from the *Pittsburgh Post-Gazette*:

"Some scientists say that if this individual is not studied further, we, as Indians, will be destroying evidence of our own history," said Armand Minthorn, an Umatilla tribal leader.

"We already know our history. It is passed on to us through our elders and through our religious practices. Scientists have dug up and studied American Indians for decades. We view this practice as desecration of the body and a violation of our most deeply held religious beliefs."

Thus, scientists are being asked to get permission from religious groups to study human remains. This is the same thing as asking an evolutionary biologist to get permission from a Christian Fundamentalists for the study of a new fossil that proves evolution occurs.

Some anthropologists and archaeologists are horrified at the prospect of the permanent loss of access to so much knowledge. Anthropologists, like Mike O'Brien, at Missouri University, Amy Dansie and Donald Tuohy, both of the Nevada State Museum, have expressed concern over the loss of scientific freedom in anthropology as a result of repatriation laws. Others have confided in me that they have been aghast at the destruction of remains when they are reburied. Some anthropologists have lamented that Native American tribes have basically told them that the study of human remains is a dead science and will soon no longer exist. Thus, whereas the American Association of Physical Anthropologists' mainstream judgment that reburial is good for anthropology may have some pragmatic merits, the case can also be made that the reburial of remains detracts from the ability of anthropologists to scientifically study humankind, which is our job.

Anthropologist Dr. Karl Reinhard, who was at the University of Nebraska, had an opportunity to experience the loss of freedom on inquiry first-hand. He conducted legitimate, high-quality scientific research on skeletal remains from prehistoric and protohistoric Nebraska Indians. He told of their lives at the point of contact over two hundred years ago. And, his work was published in the much-heralded 1994 book *In the Wake of Contact*. The December 1998 issue of the Ojibwe News covered the story of Reinhard and reported that Native Americans dissatisfied with the research conclusions sent a complaint to the university demanding the firing of Dr. Reinhard. The Native American tribe also requested repatriation of the remains and accused Dr. Reinhard of mishandling remains, which he flatly denied and filed libel suit against the Native Americans due to the harm these allegations caused his career. In the end, charges against Reinhard were dropped, but the damage had been done. He ended up moving out of the hostile environment and has since been working on South American remains. What were his offensive research objectives and conclusions, you may wonder? Reinhard, basically, examined skeletal remains through isotopic analyses, vertebral pathologies, osteoarthritis, and dental wear to determine diet and health in the pre-contact and post-contact eras of Nebraska. Reinhard found that there were both positives and negatives associated with contact with Europeans. The positives were the introduction of the horse and gun allowed more efficient hunting, which in turn provided food that is more nutritious, and also increased time and distance allotted for gathering, which increased food variety. The Native Indians, data showed, ate better after being contacted by the Europeans. On the down side, women seemed to have greater osteoarthritis in the post-contact era, which may be a result of preparing hides for fur-trading economy. The fact that looking at bones can give us an indication of health is wonderful and helps to reconstruct the past; just because these are not the desired results (I suspect the Native Americans would have liked to see that only negative results arose from contact with Europeans) does not mean the evidence should be destroyed or that the scientist should be fired.

The other way repatriation and reburial affects scientific freedom is that loss of funding means that many studies cannot be undertaken. Funding for repatriation and reburial is robust, but many funding organizations are not willing to fund anthropological endeavors requiring the study of human remains for fear that the study will not be allowed or completed. Without funds, without the support of the government (which provides some grants), without support from the academic community, and without time at our hands, osteology will die in North America. Along with this death, will be the burying of evidence to tell the true story of the Americas from the peopling of the continent to the life ways of the people who occupied the continent prior to the arrival of Europeans. When information is lost and no new evidence is gained, then the religious view from the Native Americans will gain hold and cloud up scientific understanding. Native Americans have intentionally tried to stop scientific knowledge on the peopling of the Americas. Amy Dansie in 1999 published that in Nevada, Native Americans have attempted to stop studies on Spirit Cave and Wizards Beach Man (both Paleo-Indians with no affiliation to modern Native populations). Dansie further adds that Pauite tribes have even denied the right for anthropologists to finish studies on these remains and display facial reconstructions!

A repeating theme in the repatriation literature concerns Native Americans questioning of the good that has come through the study of human remains. James Riding In in the 2000 book *Repatriation Reader* puts his expectation on anthropologists quite crudely when he recounts a story of meeting an anthropologist at a party. He suggested to the anthropologist that "if he wanted to serve Indians he should spend his time excavating latrines and leave the graves alone." Devon Mihesuah, the editor of the *Repatriation Reader*, also states one question that frequently arises is "How has the study of Indian skeletal remains helped to alleviate the problems Indians face today?" And, worse yet, Dr. Emery Johnson (one of our former Assistant Surgeon Generals) commented that he was "not aware of any current medical diagnostic or treatment procedure that has been derived from research on Indian remains."

Many tribes have decried the University of California's decision to disband NAGPRA committees since the inventories and repatriations of identifiable remains are well on their way. What's more, they claim that archaeology and anthropology is a luxury science. These individuals argue that putting the dead before the religion of the present is immoral or unethical in a luxury science. What is a luxury science; one that doesn't address issues that directly help modern indigenous populations. Science and the search for knowledge should never be considered a luxury, but a human right -- a right that may not seem to have a direct effect on people's lives, but allows them to gain the critical thinking skills and to apply these skills to their lives. So, I may never find a cure for diabetes (which plagues modern Native Americans), but I hope to give students and those who read my research knowledge that they can then use to help understand the world around them, learn how to read multiple sources and make out what people are writing about. Most importantly, I hope my students do not just accept stories (whether they be religious or other) blindly. Additionally, a society that sees science as a luxury and allows the attack of science opens the door for judgments on what is appropriate to study and what is not. It also starts to make me think that what is next; is literature a luxury too? What about art?

I am not against medical and sociological research, but I did not decide to study human remains to determine the causes of alcoholism in modern Native Americans; nor could I jump into the realm of trying to help Native Americans with these types of issues. I applaud those who have taken that course in their career, but to think that anyone who hasn't is unethical is wrong! I am the last person to argue that our science has been geared at helping to alleviate present problems or even solve medical issues. But, it has enlightened people who are interested and extends beyond the ivory towers of academia.

Bioarchaeologists work on the past and reconstructing the past; we have told the story of the past and try to continue to do so. The fact that Native Americans do not wish to hear these reconstructions is irrelevant in true science; however, it becomes relevant when science and politics mix. In other words, because of repatriation and reburial laws, scientists, such as I, have had to change research agendas to suit the desires of those in power who are the Native Americans. In order to be funded, one must do something useful for the present now in anthropology.

Knowledge for knowledge sake is important. If the Native Americans were interested in learning their true past rather than clinging on to religious ideals, then they would see how valuable our science is. Yet, if the only studies of any value are those that directly benefit modern peoples, then we can just say goodbye to whole fields of bioarchaeology, paleoanthropology (the study of human evolution), paleontology (the study of nonhuman fossils), astronomy, and many other sciences. Other scientists are not asked to fill the same as anthropologists studying prehistoric remains are asked to do. No one is asking paleoanthropologists what good does their research brings to the modern Africans. What benefit do we gain from learning about dinosaurs; does it even benefit the birds they are related to? No, those questions are not asked of others; rather their gains in knowledge are revered in magazines, such as National Geographic, and turned into television series, such as in NOVA. What their science does, which ours can too, is to give people an insight to how the world is and was. It allows children to start dreaming, not only of the future, but of the past. Knowledge is the key to a healthy life regardless of the direct benefit people seek. And, to gain knowledge, regardless of the applicability of that knowledge, is important because it leads to a more educated society. An educated society can make decisions based on truths rather than superstitions, myths, and religion. This can tie eventually into accepting that the problems of today are not due to the lack of human remains in the ground (like so many Native Americans would like you to believe).

Yet, I wonder whether they have ever considered whether their religious beliefs are their own luxuries and have not helped their peoples any more than any scientific study. Religion actually has been shown to be detrimental to people, including prayer actually hindering people from getting well (possibly due to stressing out about getting well) and giving a way to put the blame our own mistakes onto others (see Richard Dawkins' the *God Delusion*). One could turn the tables on Native Americans and ask what their oral traditions have done to alleviate their people's problems. You could even question whether the money spent on reburials, such as the $90,000 of government funds spent on the reburial of 61 Native Americans from the University of Minnesota collection reported by the *Christian Century*, could have been better spent to help those with health and mental problems in their community. Finally, I would like to know what direct benefit any reburial has had on the modern Native Americans. Have tribes who have reburied remains shown a decrease in poverty, an increase in education, or a decrease in mental health problems? These are empirical questions that can be answered. Shouldn't the Native Americans show us how repatriation has benefited their lives; where are the decreases in alcoholism, where are the increases in salaries, etc? I intend to delve into these questions at a later point in my career.

As an aside, if one really wants knowledge that can directly aid others. Forensic anthropology has been borne out of bioarchaeology. Without bioarchaeology, anthropologists would never have studied fragments of human bones to determine how individuals died, what their ages were at time of death, and how to determine sex of an individual. These studies are continued and many of them are done on prehistoric skeletal remains, but are then applied directly to crime scenes if they are found useful (such as determining new ways to age and sex an individual with bones not previously used for these identification factors). Victims who were nameless and faceless previously have now been identified due to the advances in forensic sciences. Media has been a great disseminator of the knowledge gained through forensic anthropology and each semester I have more and more students who want to specialize in forensic anthropology. These students are often unaware that forensic anthropology wouldn't exist without the study of prehistoric remains. Could this be perhaps because the media would like to avoid the link between the solving crimes and the study of prehistoric skeletal materials? Or are they just as ignorant as others who fail to see connections between skeletal material and understanding current humans?

Internationally, governments, such as Australia, have set guidelines about what research is appropriate. The types of study that should be conducted and who should conduct them are also outlined in these government guidelines. In Australia, aborigines should conduct the research and determine which questions should be asked and answered. At the very least, the government requires consultation with the aborigines (regardless of their lack of training) and the questions to ask and answer should revolve around solving problems of modern aborigines. Great Britain, also, has a research agenda outlined for anthropologists and others to help them conduct research in "important" topics of indigenous studies; all of the topics involve trying to resolve today's social problems of minority groups.

In the United States, the agenda of the government may be less obvious, but the pressure is still there. Recurrent articles and demands for returning remains unless studies actually benefit modern Native American groups are rising. Furthermore, many Native American groups deny that the reconstruction of the past is of any use to them. After all, they have their religion to tell them about their past. They also don't want any research conducted that may indicate that they are relatively late comers to the Americas (and research that suggests that they came from peoples in the Old World has been repeatedly claimed as racist). Thus, should anthropologists kowtow to Native American desires and leave the realm of the past in order to pursue benefiting the modern peoples?

Is osteology a dying science? Do my findings just suggest that studying human remains is no longer a valid way of understanding the world around us or that we have discovered all that we need to know about human remains? The answer to these questions is a resounding NO! Osteology is not a dying subject in anthropology, but rather access has declined to study Native American remains. An indication that osteology as a topic thrives comes from the annual proceedings at the American Association of Physical Anthropologists. Not only are osteology presentations the leading type of presentations in the meetings, but publications are robust as well. The overall number of osteological (this includes international and non-Native American remains) publications has increased over the last thirty years. The *American Journal of Physical Anthropology* has continued having a high percentage of osteology publications; both before and after NAGPRA, the topic most frequently published in the *American Journal of Physical Anthropology* has consistently been related to osteology and, more specifically, paleopathology (see the annual proceedings published in the December issues of the journal). Osteology is the most represented topic in the journal with around 25% of the journal's articles coming from osteological research; the next most published theme is population genetics with only around 15%. So, it does not appear that the changes are due to a decrease in interest in osteology. The increase in osteological studies not containing Native American remains, both in the *American Journal of Physical Anthropology* and other journals, such as the *International Journal of Osteoarchaeology*, lend further support to the notion that the changes documented in this report are a result of researchers avoiding remains that may be subject to NAGPRA regulations. A preliminary examination of the International Journal of Osteoarchaeology reveals that over 90% of the studies conducted on human skeletal remains in the last ten years use non-US remains. Plus, a new journal for bioarchaeology, the *International Journal of Paleopathology*, has begun publications just this year. We can only hope that this journal will have articles from both Old World and New World human remains.

It seems from the evidence that anthropologists often opt to study remains from South and Central America and Europe to avoid the complexities of repatriation issues. When I have spoken with anthropologists who conduct research abroad many have spoken of their actions outside of the United States and related their effort in part to avoid NAGPRA issues. However, the ideology of repatriation and reburial is escalating and spreading around the world as I mention earlier. Israel passed a law in 1995 that human remains must be handed over to the Ministry of Religious Affairs and not classified as "antiquities." Consequently, Haim Watzman reported in 2000 that the Hebrew University handed over numerous ancient skeletons from their research collection for reburial. Australia has passed legislation to allow Aborigines to claim prehistoric skeletons from museum collections. When skeletons are handed over, the Aborigines bury them at sea in order to ensure that scientists will never study them again. It may only be a matter of time until the same occurs in South and Central America.

Chapter 9

ETHICAL DILEMMAS

"Archaeologists who accept these situations or treat them as merely local concerns (apparently the position of most scholarly organizations, including the Society for American Archaeology), have not just compromised, they have abandoned scholarly ethics in favor of being "respectful and sensitive" to nonscholars and anti-intellectuals. When the current round of controversy is over, this loss of scientific integrity will be heavily condemned."

Clement Meighan (2000: Some Scholars Views on Reburial.
In the Repatriation Reader).

SCIENTISTS' VIEWS

What is science and what do scientists do? Science is the search for answers using data; we use the scientific method to understand the world around us, which includes the past. Religion is based on faith, which involves believing certain things to be true (such as creation stories). You cannot have faith and at the same time question your beliefs. Consequently, to be religious means to view the world through a faith based system.

Science is the opposite; it is a system based on questions and doubt. We are not asking individuals to believe anything, but rather question everything. Then, we search for the answers to the questions through the use of data, which in my case are the skeletal remains. Often times I am asked whether I believe in God, aliens, or other such things. My reply is always the same. I don't believe in anything, I think about certain things, I suspect certain things may or may not be true, but belief is not based on inquiry. So, no I don't believe in God, but I don't believe in evolution either. I think that the evidence for evolution shows that it is true. This is what science is about.

Science is also not based only on opinions, but rather the analysis of information. We use the data to tell a story and that story may vary because all the pieces are never there; the variation often depends on one's academic pedigree (which can be understood to be an informed opinion). Thus, the telling of the past by anthropologists is not empty of opinions, but it is not opinion alone. Considering how scientists approach the world, we can now understand what a scientist does.

Scientists are trained to ask and answer questions to explain things about our past, present, and to make predictions about our future using facts. Scientists ask questions, which we call hypotheses, and then explain how they will try to answer the questions. A hypothesis is not just an educated guess, as so many people classify it, rather it is a question formed from observation and formulated in a way that it is able to be answered it. Although, the question is answerable, it can be that any particular study may fail to answer. You cannot answer whether something doesn't exist (because there is always the possibility that we just haven't seen it yet). We can, conversely, answer whether something does exist. The data is then collected and we answer the question. For example, were men walking more (perhaps to hunt) than women in prehistoric populations? For my Master's thesis I decided to look at the cross-sections of thigh bones taken with a CT-scanner to examine whether the bones of males in a particular prehistoric California hunter-gatherer population were shaped differently than females; a long cross-section is said to be indicative of resisting stresses placed on thigh bones when walking and a round cross-section is indicative of sedentary behavior. I did find a sex difference and male cross-sections were less round than those of females; thus, I stated that the difference exists. Then, I can tell the story of what caused these differences, which would be women staying close to a home base collecting food while men traveled to hunt game. My story should be based on other research, ethnographic data, and biological information on bones and muscle use. Others may disagree with my reconstruction, but the data would be the same.

Because scientists are trained in the scientific method (that I just covered), we have a different ethical dilemma in regards to repatriation and reburial. I don't think that all anthropologists are aware of the ethical dilemma we face as a scientific field of study. Yet, everyone seems to be aware of the ethical considerations of repatriation and reburial from the Native American view, which I will address shortly. And, anthropologists, such as Dr. Jerome Rose and his colleagues may be correct in stating that NAGPRA has created a more ethical science. As stated earlier, even the American Association of Physical Anthropologists seems unaware of the issues at hand when dealing with human remains.

How I see it is that as scientists it is our ethical obligation to study and try to explain the world around us. And, NAGPRA and other repatriation laws obstruct the process of scientific endeavors; thereby, creating an ethical dilemma for scientists. Therefore, I think that the scientists' ethics (which is just another way of saying a set of right principles) should involve honesty and a search for the most truthful and correct explanation of the world. Honesty is an important aspect of ethics; I have been accused of equating the two, but they are deeply entwined in my worldview. Many who support Native American creation stories do not believe in a real truth or the concept of honesty. Thus, truth and honesty becomes divorced from their sense of right and wrong (or their ethics). If one doesn't value honesty, then how can we believe them when they make claims of affiliation or are reporting a wrong doing by current researchers? Perhaps this is why so many liberals who support repatriation and reburial do not accept that it is truly a religious issue even when the Native Americans claim it is. Nonetheless, to many people honesty is one of the first things they teach their children and punish them for lying; just recently, a professor at my university was saying how she grounded her child for lying about homework since lying was wrong. As a scientist, honesty is important in how we collect our data, analyze it, and finally report our results. To follow what is right, is to be an honest scientist, which hopefully leads to the best and most accurate way of understanding the world. But, it goes further, truthful reconstruction of the past or the true nature of explaining things is a matter of ethics. Anything that obstructs this task, such as accepting myths of origins, not challenging stories that we know to be false, and allowing others to propagate their myths (at the cost of our science) has to be considered unethical.

Although it sometimes feels as if I am alone in the above stated opinion, not all anthropologists are in favor of NAGPRA and these anthropologists sometimes mention the ethical dilemmas at hand for scientists. Most anthropologists take a moderate view; Dr. Philip Walker includes three ethical principles that anthropologists should follow:

> 1) human remains should be treated with dignity and respect; 2) descendants should have the authority to control the disposition of their relative's remains; and 3) because of the importance of human remains for their understanding of our common past, human remains need to be preserved when possible so that they are available for scientific research.

I would agree with the first and third of these principles. As mentioned earlier, I have the utmost respect for human remains and I try to instill that into my students. I would slightly alter the third principle; I would avoid using the term common past because it suggests that some pasts are not common. And, suggesting that there is a difference between a common past and a not common past begs the question of whether we are only entitled to learn about our own past? I would say that knowledge should be free to everyone and not doled out per population, race, or group. Finally, the second principle, I have difficulty with, of course. How close of a relative should the remains be? I could see the argument being made for immediate family (although I would have no qualms about having my parents remains used in science without my consent). How can we determine descendants when oral tradition has equal weight as scientific information? Either the law should be changed to be specific about true relationships and the generations that are included or we need to let go of this principle. I am for letting go of it. After all, according to Walker ethical values are not incorrect or correct and thus to exclude that principle will strengthen the resolve towards science and make a statement. Other anthropologists take a less moderate view than Walker does on repatriation.

Anthropologists, such as Geoffrey Clark in a 1999 *Skeptical Inquirer*, take a hard line on the science versus religion in their ethos. Clark, for instance, affirms that he thinks that archaeology and anthropology need to follow the scientific method and states that science is based on questions. Additionally, he states that the key problem with NAGPRA is that it puts science and religion on equal footing. Other state laws, such as California laws, put science a step below religion. Clement Meighan in the *Repatriation Reader* addressed some issues about scientific versus nonscientific ethics. He pointed out that the Society for American Archaeology has general goals, which include dedication to scholarly research that "require honest reporting and preservation of the evidence." Meighan made it clear that with these goals in mind, which are ethical considerations, one cannot also be in favor of reburials. He suggested that anthropologists have caved in to too many requests and have fallen into the trap of being too understanding of the other viewpoint. The Native American activists are not trying to see our point of view and are openly anti-science; accordingly, should we not be openly pro-science without the apologies that go along with our field. Many times museums have handed over collections without a fight rather than try to negotiate with Native Americans; the term sacred needs only to be applied and museum and university officials often get weak willed; whereas, they aren't even likely to believe in the sacred!

In Meighan's 2000 chapter in the *Repatriation Reader*, the ACPAC association is highlighted as one of the strong centers of anti-reburial groups. ACPAC is the American Committee for Preservation of Archaeological Collections and has been in the forefront of arguing that archaeology is a legitimate and useful profession. The past doesn't belong just to those who are distantly related to the human remains; often times

> "museum material five thousand years old are claimed by people who imagine themselves to be somehow related to the collections in question, but such a believe has no basis in evidence and is mysticism."

The American Committee for Preservation of Archaeological Collections has over 600 members in nearly all states combined. These individuals need to become even more active in protecting the remains, especially in order to protect scientific inquiry.

NATIVE AMERICAN VIEWS

From the many correspondence and interactions I have had with Native Americans, I feel that I can say something about their point of view. I have been accused of thinking that the Native Americans do not feel strongly about the skeletal remains, but, on the contrary, I am quite sure that their fight for reburial and repatriation is sincere. I think that their actions are filled with the same passion as are other religious zealots (or political activists for that matter). Just because I do not agree with their perspective does not mean that I cannot understand their perspective.

First and foremost, I think that most Native Americans who actively engage in reburial and repatriation are anti-science and pro-religion. I am not saying that all Native Americans feel this way and some Native Americans are surely pro-science although I have not met these Native Americans. I keep hearing anthropologists talking about Native Americans who conduct research and are interested in their past, but I find that these same individuals are also interested in repatriation and many of the questions that they want answered serve the purpose to help them repatriate remains. In general, I agree with Jerry Springer's assessment:

> "One of the defining characteristics of repatriationism, and of its most objectionable features, is its rejection of science and other forms of scholarly research, and its replacement by oral tradition, origin myths, animism, and a polemical dismissal of all objective standards for scholarships."

As mentioned earlier, many Native American tribes believe that they have been here from the beginning of time. Their creation stories, which are just a part of their religion, have them falling from the sky, rising from the earth, or other ways magically appear in the North Americas. Initially, Native Americans were happy to find out that the human remains found in the Americas were older than previously thought. They strongly denied the link to Asia and the migration theories of science, even though it is evident to nearly everyone that they share a lot of physical features that are similar to Asians and are cold adapted populations. It seemed to them that the older finds were notable proof that scientists were wrong; Native Americans were here long before we had thought – perhaps from the beginning of time. Unfortunately, new research showed that these Paleo-Indians were not related to modern

Native Americans. This created a new rift between Native Americans and scientists. The data was an affront to their religious beliefs.

Moreover, Geoffrey Clark points out that religion is ever present in NAGPRA discussions. He calls the discussions "psychodrama" which he then defines as stuff of religious beliefs and politics; both of which (in the best of worlds) have "no place in science." Even Nani Ratnawati admits that some archaeologists disregard the spiritual significance of repatriation. I acknowledge that Native Americans have these significances, but I don't think they need to be addressed in a world where science should take precedence over religion. A California Indian who Ratnawati spoke with talked of the religious experience involved with repatriation, including journey to spirit world. Another Native American she spoke with mentions the Creator and sacredness of the remains and artifacts. Religion, I think, is the over-riding reason for repatriation.

But, it is about more than just religion. Repatriation is also about power shifts. There is no doubt that the Native American peoples were displaced with the arrival of Europeans. Natives were killed in vast numbers either intentionally or through diseases that they had no natural immunity to. Then, the remaining Native Americans were marginalized and not made citizens until 1830. Thus, they have legitimate grievances. Even now, they have the highest drug and alcohol abuse rates, domestic violence is rampant, and the highest poverty rates of all Americans (including recent immigrants)! Their college attendance is consistently low and they seem to be plagued with all sorts of social problems. Some of these problems are being addressed and money is flowing into certain tribes who have land claims; Indian casinos have been a mixed blessing for the tribes. With all these grievances, Native Americans have been in a power struggle with their white counterparts. This is true in Canada as well. Part of NAGRPA is about having a law that requires Western culture (which is in part scientific) to kowtow to Native culture, which is mostly religious. Getting scientists to ask for permission to study remains, attend feasts of respect, and marching through research corridors of museums banging drums, is not only about spirituality, but also about power. They have put us in our place; taken over our institutions (at least temporarily) and forced us to assimilate to their culture. This is a reversal of power. I wouldn't be against this reversal if it meant that we were moving toward a more rational society; I am not concerned over who has the power, but rather what that power is used for. When power is used to demand the destruction of casts in order to prevent the progress of science, then I am against those in power. Many individuals may believe that Native Americans are still at a loss of power, but in the realm of the study of human remains the tide has turned. Scientists are no longer steering the ship to tomorrow, but rather back-tracking with apologies and conducting rituals that they shouldn't be required to participate in, just as I shouldn't be required to wear a veil if Muslims asked me to or go to confession while not a Catholic!

James Riding In writes about his perspective as a Native American Pawnee Indian in *Repatriation Reader: Who Own American Indian Remains*. He makes it clear that he wishes all Native American remains to be reburied and has no regard for anthropological science. Riding In states that although he has been exposed to archaeology and other Western sciences, he would not give up his traditional religion. He considers all remains to have been stolen and cries out for repatriation and reburial of all non-white remains.

Given all this, Native American ethical considerations are not based on honesty and truth (as mine are), but rather they are faith and power based; what tells them right and wrong are their creation myths and the acceptance of others not to challenge their beliefs.

Anthropologist Nani Ratnawati points out that some Native Americans add respect to their definition of ethics; of course, this relates to archaeologists having respect for their creation stories. The Native Americans may feel insulted that anthropologists call their stories myths and point out that they are false, but to agree with these stories (and not try to educate those who we work with or for – as in the case of Native Americans and others) would be breaking the ethical code of a scientist. How can they be upset that we would call them liars, if their ethical considerations do not even include honesty? If they accept falsehoods as real and base what is right and wrong upon these falsehoods, then they cannot be considered truthful. Their passion, faith, and desire may be intact, but their ability to accept truth and honesty as being right is shattered.

Chapter 10

FUTURE OF THE STUDY OF HUMAN REMAINS

"Yet the loss of prehistoric skeletal material to science is incalculable, and that consideration should take precedence, in my view, over the religious concerns of Native Americans. The worldviews of science and religion are fundamentally incommensurate. They cannot be reconciled."

Geoffrey Clark (1999: NAGPRA, science and the demon-haunted world.
Skeptical Inquirer)

POSSIBILITY OF FUTURE STUDIES

There are always those who echo hopeful words of "we can still study the remains with permission from the Native American tribes," if Native America tribes realize the importance of the studies being conducted or the bones can be uncovered again and studied anew. However, these hopes are as childish as still believing in Santa Claus. Once human remains have been repatriated and reburied, they are gone forever.

Last year I had a Ph.D. student visit San Jose State University to study the skeletal collection available; he took measurements and did not conduct any destructive data collection. He is at one of the most prestigious universities in the world and I am sure that his dissertation will reveal much needed information about past peoples. Yet, he confided in me that he has encountered opposition to getting access to skeletal remains that have been repatriated (but not reburied) to Native American tribes. Many tribes have in place a procedure to apply for studying remains, but none grants access to the skeletal remains. He stated that his experience was not unique; in fact, there are no documented cases of a repatriated skeletal collection being studied by anthropologists. The fact is that when remains are repatriated, they are no longer available for study regardless of the research question or methods that would be employed for the studies.

Other people have mentioned that there is a possibility of studying the new remains that are unearthed with new construction sites, but the new state laws that are being enacted prevent studying of remains further than figuring out affiliation without the tribal consent. This means that anthropologists have to work to figure out affiliation, but cannot use any of this time to also conduct their own research, regardless of whether it is destructive or not. Perhaps by the time affiliation is determined, the tribe most closely associated with the skeletal remains will not okay research. I find it demeaning that anthropologists cannot conduct their work without getting the nod of approval by many individuals who have no regard for science. The anti-science sentiment is fervent in many tribal communities. Their religious beliefs do not require them to understand their past through science, just as the Christian fundamentalists do not need scientists to explain the world around them. So, the possibility of future studies shrinks with each new law that is enacted and each discovery made. Anthropologists may turn into drones answering the same questions over and over again – affiliation, sex, and age!

WHEN BONES ARE REBURIED: DESTRUCTION OF HUMAN REMAINS

The other situation that of bones that have been reburied is far more dismal. Prehistoric skeletal remains are often fragile. We are fortunate to have so many remains that have been carefully excavated and are in good condition at my university; yet, this is often not the case. Furthermore, even when the skeletal remains are in good condition while they are curated at a university or a museum in non-acidic boxes, temperature controlled rooms, and vermin-free environments, their preservation will be destroyed as soon as they are placed back into the ground. An anthropologist colleague of mine who works in the public sector of archaeology has described to me the horror of reburying remains. She said that once the boxes are placed into the ground and dirt is placed on top of them, you could hear the bones starting to break and crack. This is especially true for baby and child remains that are so valuable to anthropologists to understand health of prehistoric populations. One can just imagine the sound of these little bones being destroyed by the ground that is meant to preserve their ancestral lineages.

The tribe most likely associated with the remains at San Jose State University runs an archaeological firm and recovers skeletal remains at construction sites; the Muwekma-Ohlone Native Americans have no qualms, supposedly, regarding the study of human remains and they have their folks and ours study the remains after they are uncovered. However, this same tribe reburies the remains as soon as the initial data is collected. One must ask where their allegiances truly are; can they be pro-science and pro-reburial at the same time? When the bones are reburied, do they feel the same horror at the sound of data destruction as I would? I can only guess that they do not or they would start a repository for these remains for anthropologists and themselves to conduct continuous scientific research to help understand the past lives of their ancestors. Currently, the Muwekma-Ohlone tribe has no federal recognition and, thus, have no legal claims on the skeletons housed at San Jose State University. Yet, the department of anthropology has kept a strong relationship with the tribe and we work together on many projects. An adjunct faculty member who works for San Jose State University and sometimes teaches courses in archaeology is working with the Muwekma-Ohlone in order to get them federal recognition. Although, his intentions may be honorable, I would suggest that there is a conflict of interest. If he were a true scientist, then why would he aid in the possible loss of data? When and if the Muwekma-Ohlone gain federal recognition, they may decide to repatriate the remains. They have previously and continue to rebury remains; the thought of losing the excellent skeletal collection housed at

San Jose State University makes my heart sink. I wonder where the Muwekma-Ohlone will stand if their status of recognition changes.

Going back to the destruction of remains, I ask myself, could I rebury human remains? My answer is no and my opinion is that anthropologists whose lives are intertwined with those of the past to bring a voice to prehistory have an ethical obligation not to rebury remains. By taking part in reburial rituals, we break our ethical code as scientists. We are saying that it is okay to destroy remains and that reburial is ethical for ourselves. Even repatriation becomes an ethical breach for scientists since Native American groups do not allow for the study of these remains.

At the Canadian Museum of Civilization, the reburial of Haida skeletal remains was coupled with a feast of respect. Curators and other museum officials were required to attend this ceremony to show respect for the Native Canadians and presumably their remains. On the other hand, how can an anthropologist sincerely attend such a ritual when it goes against the ethos of science to destroy evidence for the sake of religion? Did the Haida really think that this would bring respect or was it a means to show the power shift? It is hard to say what the intentions were, but participating in these activities says that it is okay to destroy our science and it isn't.

Recently, San Francisco State University has had to remove their human remains and house them in facilities belonging to the Native American Studies Program. My Master's students have tried to gain access to those remains for their theses, which all include nondestructive data collection methods. Initially, our email and phone requests to gain access were ignored. Then, after much effort, I finally got an email from the anthropologist in charge who said that skeletal collections were off limits currently. It appears that the people in the Native American Studies Program would not allow for research on the skeletal remains. The Muwekma-Ohlone tribe who claim to be the ancestors of these remains has tried to step in and aid my students. They wrote to individuals who were curating the San Francisco collection saying that they had no problems with the study of the remains. This seems like a noble act and perhaps my students will gain access to the remains; however, it seems demeaning that anthropologists with Ph.D.s who have made it their career to understand the past have no say in whether these curated remains will be studied. Remember that the Muwekma-Ohlone have no legal claims to be able to grant access to the collection and, plus, these are the same group of people who rebury remains on a regular basis and claimed more than 550 skeletal remains from the collection at San Jose State University right before NAGPRA was to be passed! They reburied those remains and reduced our sample size. Why would they have more authority than anthropologists would at San Francisco State University (who housed those remains for decades)? Why is their word more valuable than my own? Does being a Native American give them some special privilege or does it mean that they know more about the study of human remains than a person who has a Ph.D. with a specialty in osteology? Finally, are their ethical concerns more valid than those of scientists?

Can We Get Along:
Collaboration with Scientists and Native Americans?

Can we get along? Is it possible that scientists and Native Americans will collaborate to a full extent? I don't know the answer to these questions. Many anthropologists have said that it is possible and even occurring. In principle, it occurs at the university where I am located, but I am not sure that this is a truly balanced collaboration. From all that I have read, collaboration basically involves anthropologists conceding to the Native Americans in situations where repatriation has yet to occur. Sometimes this involves taking part in Native rituals. I remember my first experience in field school through Cabrillo Community College (which is close to Monterey Bay south of San Francisco). We were excavating a Native American site at Big Sur for the government who wanted to improve parking and bathroom facilities on a gorgeous beach location. Cabrillo Community College was hired by the government to do the excavation to ensure that the site was not a burial ground. It turned out that the only things of interest that we found were a couple of broken arrowheads. What I remember most about this experience is the complete embarrassment I felt when the Native American who was required to be onsite led us into Native American rituals, such as circle dances and songs. I also remember his lectures on spirituality, which I just thought were sermons. These things turned me off to field school. I didn't become an anthropologist to be religious and I felt his practices were a religious intrusion on archaeological field school (which was being paid for in part by the government). Some people may think that I am being unreasonable, but let us imagine that we would be asked to take part in Catholic rituals when doing fieldwork in Italy or veiling ourselves when doing fieldwork in the Middle East. I don't wish for others to teach me their religions while I am getting my education. Isn't this the same as teaching Intelligent Design in the classroom? Using the same reasoning, if religion continues to permeate through the Native American's perspective of collaboration, then I would say no we shouldn't collaborate and that collaboration is unethical.

Other collaborations that I have yet to experience, but have read about include concessions of when to work on remains. In 2005, the *American Journal of Physical Anthropology* published an article by Dr. Stephen Ousley and colleagues that addressed many issues surrounding repatriation and reburial. Ousley works at the Smithsonian in Washington D.C. with a large skeletal collection. In the article, the authors talk about concessions made to Native Americans after consultation. Some of these concessions include the need to "'feed' human remains by leaving pollen, tobacco, or foodstuffs nearby." Since museums usually try to avoid having food in curation facilities (to prevent bugs and rodents from entering the locations), curators have actually placed the offerings in plastic containers to meet the "spiritual need" for feeding the remains. Other unnecessary activities include only handling warriors in the early morning or facing all the skulls east. Additionally, some requests have required separate rooms with special ventilation systems, such as "in the for ritual smudging, or other forms of burning." These requests, whether they are easy to follow or require extensive time and money, are done for religious purposes. They take time out of research and they restrict some studies. It is unfathomable to me that the US government and some of the brightest minds in anthropology support and follow through with these requests. I cannot understand how an educated individual who is trained in anthropology could be so accommodating when they are not so in other instances. Ousley and his co-workers don't write about these requests as being unreasonable, instead they seem to think that they are ethical ways of dealing with skeletal remains and their affiliated tribes. For example, they state:

> "Tribal visitors also inform us as to how the remains can be treated properly while the remains are curated at the museums. Most traditional-care requests are readily accommodated through creative collections management…All of these requests were easily accommodated…These traditional-care requests include specifications of specialized housing, indicating appropriate objects that can or should be stored with the remains, providing a covering such as red cloth, and facilitating access for feeding, ceremonies, or prayers."

The number of times religion comes up in these issues is astounding, yet anthropologists and other scientists seem accepting of this religious intrusion.

More worrisome still is the way the collaboration shapes the questions anthropologists ask and answer about human remains. I was sitting at the annual San Jose State University student competition watching two of my students present their research on violence and the prehistoric collection housed at our university when I witnessed what I thought to be a totally inappropriate question asked by one of the judges. She asked whether they had obtained permission to conduct this research from the affiliated tribe (to no other presenter had they asked whether they had obtained special permissions or gone through the internal review board process). What was even more shocking was that my students (who were remaining students from my predecessor at the University and had actually conducted the research prior to my starting to work at San Jose State University) had actually asked the "affiliated" tribe for permission to conduct the research. It appears that this was the standard procedure for research prior to my taking the helm of physical anthropology at San Jose State University. Why this is so shocking is that the tribe they seek permission from is not federally recognized and, thus, have no claim to these remains. Furthermore, there have been no conclusive scientific studies to determine affiliation. Finally, does this mean that certain types of research questions cannot be asked?

Some Native American tribes have an interest in prehistoric life ways, but the most commonly asked questions refer to aging and sexing of individuals (and sometimes status of individuals) in order to conduct appropriate reburials. You see, many tribes have different burial rituals and methods for males and females and varying age groups. This type of research provides very little for answering questions of scientific value. Other information that Native Americans are interested may revolve around DNA analysis to try to find a direct genetic link between the past and the present peoples. Yet, these analyses are often requested of unaffiliated remains in hopes of determining affiliation and, thus, claiming the remains for reburial. Native Americans are not trying to determine whether the remains with a loose affiliation may not be affiliated and, thus, the DNA analyses are usually not requested in these cases.

Analyses of diseases, such as syphilis or tuberculosis, are not requested even though this type of research may help determine the origin of the diseases and, therefore, tell us whether they were brought to the New World by Europeans or visa versa. Also, indicators of violence, sacrifice, and cannibalism are never desired topics and Native Americans often try to deny their violent pasts of their claimed ancestors. As well, osteological analyses of crania are not popular as a way of determining affiliation when other evidence (as weak as the evidence may be) exists. Should anthropologists be dictated by the desires of Native American religious fanatics? Should we conduct research in order to help Native American's rebury the human remains properly or should we ask questions that address issues yet to be resolved?

Since having taken over the position at San Jose State University as physical anthropologist, I do not require my students or other students to okay their research proposals by the Muwekma-Ohlone and I do not ask for permission for certain studies either. My research, and I hope that all research is conducted this way, is based on the desire to learn the truth about prehistoric peoples. I am fully aware that some truths may not have desirable outcomes. Plus, there is always a possibility that someone else could retest what has been already done to provide replicable results or negate the previous findings. That is science. I do not wish to be an assistant to reburial practices and conduct research only in order to aid people to perform religious ceremonies correctly. Even when Native American tribes have a true interest in the past, if they also engage in these religious activities, then they cannot understand science. Science is about replication and how can studies be replicated if the data is lost. Using science to support religion of any sort is counter-productive.

Dr. Vincas Steponaitis, who is the director of the Research Laboratories of Archaeology at the University of North Carolina and also a member of the NAGPRA Review Committee, has been quoted by *Indian Country Today* in May 2007 as saying "Ninety-nine percent of what happens under NAGPRA is consensual and amicable. Basically, tribes and museums are working together now under NAGPRA." Is this true? Where did he get this figure? Research on NAGPRA shows that not only is there a lot of disagreement between scientists and Native American groups, but that even Native Americans often disagree. Furthermore, has the collaboration gone in both directions? I suggest in this section that there have been collaborations, but they involve anthropologists making the compromises and these are sometimes in conflict with being an ethical scientist.

James Riding In has a Native American perspective on collaboration that many anthropologists would not like to admit is alive and well. Riding In is an anti-scientific Native American who believes all Native American remains (regardless of affiliation or temporal periods) should be buried and never studied. He further adds that he does not need science to tell him about his peoples, culture, and religion (which is obtained through oral tradition, dreams, and research). Most importantly, Riding In makes it perfectly clear that collaboration beyond handing over remains is undesirable. He views the advent of archaeological programs among Native Americans as negative and dismisses the idea that they can learn about their past through archaeology. He perceives these attempts as a way for archaeologists to "adopt less abrasive tactics to get their hands on our dead." Unfortunately, he is not alone in this viewpoint.

Another point of view among Native Americans is that collaboration is possible. The Hopi, for example, have been actively collaborating with anthropologists in projects that have uncovered human remains, such as dam work, gas pipeline constructions, and mining activities. Kurt Dongoske in the 2000 the *Repatriation Reader* writes about these collaborations. He points out that often Native Americans are eager for certain osteological analyses to be conducted, such as sex, age, and disease determinations. Also, some are even interested in knowing genetic information to reconstruct their migration patterns. But, once again, it is the Native Americans determining the questions to be asked and answered and not giving anthropologists the leeway to ask further questions if desired. Additionally, Dongoske admits that the reburial of the skeletal remains is essential and that only several months are allowed for study of the more unusual collections. Other collections, however, cannot be studied outside of the field, which makes true scientific research impossible. Fortunately, casts would be allowed in order to study dentition, which may aid in the drawing of family trees. Casts, nevertheless, are less accurate and more expensive than the remains themselves and, as a result, can put anthropologists at a quandary. Finally, although the Hopi's have been more generous and more in favor of studies than many other tribes (see the Pawnee perspective mentioned above), they still hold the reins and anthropologists are turned into application driven professionals rather than inquiry based scientists. As an aside, Dongoske doesn't fail to mention the sins of past anthropologists and uses the past to imply the generosity of current Native Americans in their collaboration with anthropologists.

Another example of collaboration comes from Dr. Larry Zimmerman's review of osteologist Colin Pardoe's work in Australia. Pardoe makes a point of conducting research with community involvement; before anything starts, the Aborigines are invited to participate, even if the bones are likely to be unrelated to the modern tribes. Pardoe consults the community about research questions; he asks permission to conduct research and he even asks for permission if the human remains are unlikely to be related to the community. Furthermore, Pardoe admits that his research questions have become limited, but he accepts this cost. Whereas, others are not willing to accept the cost of limiting the types of questions that one wishes to ask. If the question is politically hot or perhaps could put Native peoples in a bad light, would permission be granted? What if I wish to ask questions about inbreeding, violence, and most importantly ancestry? Has it come to the point that the only questions that are acceptable are questions that are okayed by a nonscientific committee? Some have argued that in the realm of prehistory, freedom of scientific inquiry has become buried with the onset of repatriation and reburial laws.

Daryll Stapp, an anthropologist working in Cultural Resource Management in Washington State, claims that the involvement of Native Americans in anthropology has had positive effects. One of these effects includes dissemination of knowledge, which I am very much for. Getting knowledge to as many minds as possible is a highly valued ethic for me as a scientist. However, the knowledge should be based on the scientific method and on analyses of data. This knowledge also shouldn't be tinted with political agendas, as the Native Americans who opposed Reinhard's findings revealed. Furthermore, the opposition of full study or any study that may upset religious beliefs has been a continuous battle in collaborative work, especially when one considers the value NAGPRA has placed on religion. On the other side, Stapp states that "archaeology has been infused with new ideas through its contact with tribes and exposure to tribal perspectives." I wonder which new ideas and what perspectives Stapp is considering in his research? Has he included oral traditions that we know to be lacking substance after a few generations? Or has he also embraced the religious views of the Native Americans as we were exposed to in Cabrillo Community College Field School?

Another example of collaboration comes from Dr. Kent Lightfoot an archaeologist at University of California, Berkeley. He talks of the importance of including Native Americans in research and fieldwork in a 2006 edition of News from Native California. His collaborative field school holds lectures in the evening on oral traditions and religion. Moreover, he clearly states that Native Americans are consulted on the research plan; and, thus, their religious observances are considered seriously. In other words, they have the final word in field and research practices. Most disturbing to me, a female, is that the Native Americans Lightfoot works with have strict taboos involving the menstrual cycle. Women cannot work while they are menstruating, they also cannot participate in ceremonies, or prepare foods since they are considered unclean during this time! Lightfoot obliges discrimination against women because of these religious fanatics; if he worked with Muslims would he oblige their anti-female requests as well? Furthermore, he jokes about how the Native Americans had a lock down because he accidentally put his wife's dishes with others while she was menstruating. He states "the Kashaya elders were not amused. The word on the North Coast is that Lightfoot has a long way to go before he makes the transformation into a real man." Is it obligatory to inform everyone in camp when one is menstruating? Isn't this a private matter and involving everyone can be embarrassing to our own culture, but the Native American religion takes precedent? And, what other forms of discrimination are accepted or will be accepted? What if the Native Americans were to have religious rules about homosexuals; would these anthropologists then engage in other forms of discrimination? Kent Lightfoot refers to his experiences in a light-hearted manner, but underneath lies the cold truth that the Native Americans he works with are discriminatory and not accepting of cultural variation. Lightfoot claims that Native Americans can provide a "sensitivity training for both non-Indians and young Natives raised off the reservation." Shouldn't we rather be focused on providing a scientific (or at least methodological) training in field school; it isn't bible camp or some kind of Chinese communist training ground. I cannot understand how these individuals can justify their actions.

CONCLUDING STATEMENTS

NAGPRA has been bad for science. It deters people from working on Native American remains, it costs millions of dollars, and it consumes millions of hours that could be devoted to understanding the past better. A huge number of skeletal remains have been reburied; these are no longer available for study. Another large amount has been repatriated, but still is off limits for scientists. Then, there are those that are in the process of being removed, which makes them unavailable for study as well. My greatest fear is that the collections will eventually all disappear and the science of osteology will go by the wayside as well. The attempts to rebury unaffiliated remains may just go through and, thus, another large percentage of data will be lost. New collections are not being formed due to laws that prevent keeping bones and excavating new remains.

The passing of laws to halt the progress of science is not over. The federal government is currently examining ways that NAGPRA can be more effective in removing skeletal materials from scientists. For example, they are looking into what kind of action should be taken when remain are not claimed; such as regulation number 43 CFR 10.7 that seeks to address "disposition of unclaimed human remains, funerary objects, sacred objects, or objects of cultural patrimony." In other words, we may soon have a regulation in place that is meant to remedy the "problem" of a failure to repatriate remains where no claim has been made!

Another new regulation being considered is numbered 43 CFR 10.11 and deals with the treatment of culturally unidentifiable human remains. This sections will help dispose of remains that have no identifiable modern counterpart. The NAGPRA website states that:

"Key issues to be addressed include determining who may make a claim for culturally unidentifiable human remains, under what circumstances transfer may take place, and reporting requirements."

Matthew Daily of the Associated Press has stated in a 2007 news article that scientists continue to protest these changes and "for the third time in four years, the scientists oppose a Senate bill that would allow federally recognized tribes to claim ancient remains even if they can't prove a link to a certain tribe." This new law would end even the study of remains like Kennewick Man. The Bush Administration "called the proposed changes too broad" and they have stated that the changes would "loosen the Indian graves law to include remains that might not be connected to a tribe." Senator Doc Hastings has noted that this new Senate bill is an effort for the Senate to "extinguish scientific research" and "has to be challenged." Even the American Association of Physical Anthropologists has made a strong statement against the repatriation of culturally unidentifiable human remains. The 2007 statement includes that:

> these burdensome and ill-conceived regulations would result in a disastrous loss of unique and irreplaceable information that will forever hobble our understanding of the heritage shared by all people. The extra-legal regulatory mechanism devised in these proposed regulations—automatically giving museum collections to any culturally unaffiliated groups who express an interest in them—is not only inconsistent with the key goal of NAGPRA, but it is also ethically repugnant. It will rob all future generations of historical information on the human condition that our descendents will need to meet the many difficult future challenges the members of our species will undoubtedly be forced to confront.

Interestingly, at the same time the new NAGPRA regulations have been put forth Native Americans have attacked one of California's most prestigious institutions, University of California at Berkeley, for mistreating Native American remains. Native Americans are taking umbrage at the decision that 12,000 human remains could not be culturally identified and are being housed at the university. Thus, they have protested and the National Congress of American Indians, which is the largest national organization of American Indians, has called for an investigation into whether the university has violated NAGPRA. Even with new regulations and new attacks, some things never change. The Native Americans leading the attack against Berkeley have no interest in learning about their past. They, like so many other Native Americans, claim to once again know where they come from. Lalo Franco of the Tachi Yokut tribe states that "there is no need for science to study their ancestors' bones to prove that their people originally walked across a land bridge from Asia." Franco, instead, believes the Yokut creation myth that says that they were always in the San Joaquin Valley. In a *Los Angeles Times* article by journalist Richard Paddock, Franco is quoted as saying, "They dismiss our stories and say that what we believe are myths, but for us they are the truths of how we came out. If they want to know who we are, they can ask us."

We have seen through the chapters how repatriation and reburial negatively affects science. I have demonstrated how laws supporting repatriation are a break in the separation of Church and State. I have also argued that there are more than just the religious ethics of the Native Americans or even their supporters (whether they are on the left or right side of the political spectrum). There is a scientific ethic based on honesty and a duty to ask and answer questions. The future for the science of anthropological studies of the past looks grim.

In California, CalNAGPRA will start to empty the university and museums of prehistoric remains whether there is a clear biological link or not. Additionally, a bill is currently pending in the California legislature that Attorney Alan Schneider states on Friends of America's Past website could end the scientific endeavors of archaeology and bioarchaeology in the field. Senate Bill Number 18 is a bill that would like to add a new classification called "Traditional Tribal Cultural Site." Basically, this would mean that all archaeological sites that are on public land could become off limits to scientists by being classified as a tribal site. These sites could not be utilized without the consent of tribes. "Traditional Tribal Cultural Sites" will be defined as "a site that is traditionally associated with, or has served as the site for engaging activities related to, the traditional beliefs, cultural practices, or ceremonies of a Native American tribe." In other words, nearly any site that they wish to claim will be off limits to archaeologists; this could mean that the only field archaeology Californians will be able to engage in is that where construction requires an archaeologist present.

We are turning scientists into laborers who are not able to answer the questions that drew them into the field in the first place. Furthermore, with this new bill, human remains found on public land must be reburied in a location where they will not be rediscovered even if there is no descendent! Fortunately, the law has not passed, but was mighty close with just a veto from then governor Gray Davis saving archaeology. Perhaps next time we will not be so lucky.

But, California is not the only place in danger of losing archaeological science. A similar federal law is pending. The Native American Sacred Lands Act attempts to ban activities on all lands that are considered sacred due to traditional culture or religious reasons according to Friends of America's Past website. Some of the scary features of this bill include using the term "Native Science" as opposed to oral traditions and stating that the "Native Science" must be given the same weight (or more) than other evidence. Thus, oral traditions, which we know to be mutable, are given the same weight as biological evidence, such as DNA or skeletal morphology (which we know not to be mutable). And, people who are not directly connected to the site have no standing to contest decisions; hence, if this had been the case in Kennewick Man's discovery, the scientists who filed the suit against the government to prevent inappropriate repatriation would have no legal right to do so under the new legislation. Finally, the information from the hearings will not be publicly available through the Freedom of Information Act due to religious sensitivities; therefore, we will never know which decisions were based on facts and which were based on myths.

What do these two legislations mean for the greater picture? As anthropologists get better and better at determining the past and recording it as much more complicated with many migrations and groups being extinct and modern Native Americans not relating to all past populations, we get less and less control and our words become bastardized. By using terms such as "Native Science," science becomes just another word. The "Native Science" that they are referring to is not science at all, but by saying it is makes their myths have more weight than previously. Calling Intelligent Design a scientific theory does not make it so and unless Intelligent Design and Native American oral stories go through the scientific process, then they cannot be sciences. To throw around the term science makes real science seem meaningless! We are losing the battle even though our science is getting better and better.

But, the news is not all bad. The NAGPRA amendment I mentioned earlier proposed by Senator John McCain, which would have changed the definition of Native American from "Of, or relating to, a tribe, people, or culture that is indigenous to the United States" to "Of, or relating to, a tribe, people, or culture that was indigenous to the United States" did not pass. One interesting little facet of this amendment was that McCain tried to pass it off as a technical note change in order to make it pass more quickly. Fortunately, anthropologists and others stepped up and opposed this change. The American Association of Physical Anthropologists opposed the change initially, but than took a moderate turn and sat on the fence. Unfortunately, the bill has surfaced again and the Senate Indian Affairs Committee approved it; hopefully, the Bush administration will again oppose it.

Congressman Doc Hastings, a Republican from Washington State, decried the fact that it took a decade for Kennewick Man to be free for scientific study. He strongly opposed the amendment put forth by McCain and put forth an amendment of his own, which was supported by the American Association of Physical Anthropologists. In his 2006 press release, Hastings said "This will make it crystal clear that ancient remains should be studied by scientists and not automatically turned over to the tribes." Hastings's bill would clarify the Native American Graves Protection and Repatriation Act (NAGPRA) by requiring substantial scientific study and good evidence of relatedness with the human remains and the modern Native populations with includes genetic and cultural evidence, but excludes geographical connections. Furthermore, Hastings's bill would protect the availability of scientific studies by insuring that:

> "Nothing in this Act shall be deemed to restrict excavation, examination, investigation, or scientific study under the Archeological Resources Protection Act of 1979 of any cultural item found on Federal land that has not been determined to be the property of an Indian tribe or a Native Hawaiian organization."

Whether this bill passes has yet to be determined. Native Americans and other groups are actively seeking petition signers to prevent the passing of this bill. Matt Zimmerman, who is the Program Associate for the Dialogue Between Science and Religion at American Association for the Advancement of Science, has noted that while this bill "was welcomed by many anthropologists and archeologists, Native American interests felt that it ceded too much decision making authority to science and that it violated the balance established in NAGPRA." He opposes the bill and emphasizes that NAGPRA was established with seeing both the scientific and religious evidence as being legitimate in repatriation claims. His opinion is that the Kennewick Man case wasn't resolved sooner due to a lack of appropriate implementation of NAGPRA rather than a fault in how the law was written.

The ever-broadening definition of Native American was momentarily halted and others have attempted to protect scientific actions. The Federal government has also sided with scientists (albeit after long battles) with Kennewick Man and, at least in part, with Spirit Cave Man. Being a prehistoric skeleton is not enough to be defined Native American. However, these are protective of only a hand-full of skeletal remains -- those fascinating Paleo-Indians. Other human remains are still at risk for repatriation and this risk may extend to unidentifiable remains shortly. State laws may also increase the loss of materials, especially in key states, such as California.

Thus, even though some scientists, such as anthropologists Anthony Klesert and Shirley Powell paint a rosier picture on the ethics involved in repatriation and suggest that "the rights of those being studied take precedence over the rights of anthropologists who study them," there are others who have similar concerns as myself. I would say that if I were actually studying living humans, then Powell and Klesert would be correct, but I am not studying the modern Native Americans and, as a result, the peoples I am studying are deceased and cannot have their rights accessed. I am not alone in the dire predictions that are put forth in this book; Clement Meighan in *Repatriation Reader* highlighted some of the extremism in the anti-archaeological field. He suggested that the first actions of Native Americans were modest, but that goals are becoming more aggressive and that the desire for Native Americans invested in reburial is to put archaeologists out of business. Christopher Quayle, who is an attorney for the three affiliated tribes, is quoted as saying "It's conceivable that some time in the not-so-distant future there won't be a single Indian skeleton in any museum in the country."

Anthropologists aided in the enactment of repatriation and reburial laws; we have worked hand-in-hand with those who have strikingly different worldviews, ethics, and agendas. When NAGPRA was enacted, the safety net of affiliation and federal recognition might have seemed enough to ensure the continuous success of anthropology along with the righting of wrongs that have been committed in the past. On the other hand, a few anthropologists clearly saw that NAGPRA was just the beginning of the loss of skeletal data. New laws are popping up to help empty our institutions from research materials. Amendments to NAGPRA are being proposed to allow for more and more repatriation to occur. Our options are dwindling; we can hope for the passing of Hastings's Law to deter unaffiliated remains from being buried. We can also study remains in other countries; that is, until the reburial movement takes hold in these locations. We can prolong our studies and fieldwork through compromising our ethical values and following religious acts of others; thereby, participating in foolishness at best and discrimination at worst. Or, we can fight the good fight and try to have bad laws, like NAGPRA, repealed. We can educate the public and students about science and how it is not reconcilable with religion. Without compromise, we may have a war, but there is at least a chance of winning rather than our slow surrender. After all, Native American activists (with religious fervor) have been on the warpath to end the scientific study of prehistoric human remains and have been making progress on their front at the cost of our scientific lives.

Appendix A

USEFUL WEBSITES

American Anthropological Association	http://www.aaanet.org
American Association of Physical Anthropologists	http://www.physanth.org
Friends of America's Past	http://www.friendsofpast.org
Society for American Archaeology	http://www.saa.org
Official NAGPRA page	http://www.nps.gov/history/nagpra/
US Constitution	http://www.gpoaccess.gov/constitution/index.html
United Nations	http://www.un.org
UNESCO	http://www.unesco.org
International Council of Monuments and Sites	http://www.icomos.org

NAGPRA
NATIVE AMERICAN GRAVES PROTECTION AND REPATRIATION ACT

PUBLIC LAW 101-601--NOV. 16, 1990

NATIVE AMERICAN GRAVES PROTECTION AND REPATRIATION ACT

[104 STAT. 3048 PUBLIC LAW 101-601--NOV. 16, 1990]

PUBLIC LAW 101-601
101ST CONGRESS

AN ACT

Nov.16, 1990

[H.R. 5237]

To provide for the protection of Native American graves, and for other purposes.

Be it enacted by the Senate and House of Representatives of the United States of America in Congress assembled,

Native American
Graves Protection
and Repatriation
Act. Hawaiian
Natives. Historic
preservation.
25 USC 3001
note.
25 USC 3001.

SECTION 1. SHORT TITLE.

This Act may be cited as the "Native American Graves Protection and Repatriation Act".

SEC. 2. DEFINITIONS.

For purposes of this Act, the term-

(1) "burial site" means any natural or prepared physical location, whether originally below, on, or above the surface of the earth, into which as a part of the death rite or ceremony of a culture, individual human remains are deposited.

(2) "cultural affiliation" means that there is a relationship of shared group identity which can be reasonably traced historically or prehistorically between a present day Indian tribe or Native Hawaiian organization and an identifiable earlier group.

(3) "cultural items" means human remains and-

(A) "associated funerary objects" which shall mean objects that, as a part of the death rite or ceremony of a culture, are reasonably believed to have been placed with individual human remains either at the time of death or later, and both the human remains and associated funerary objects are presently in the possession or control of a Federal agency or museum, except that other items exclusively made for burial purposes or to contain human remains shall be considered as associated funerary objects.

(B) "unassociated funerary objects" which shall mean objects that, as a part of the death rite or ceremony of a culture, are reasonably believed to have been placed with individual human remains either at the time of death or later, where the remains are not in the possession or control of the Federal agency or museum and the objects can be identified by a preponderance of the evidence as related to specific individuals or families or to known human remains or, by a preponderance of the evidence, as having been removed from a specific burial site of an individual culturally affiliated with a particular Indian tribe,

(C) "sacred objects" which shall mean specific ceremonial objects which are needed by traditional Native American religious leaders for the practice of traditional Native American religions by their present day adherents, and

(D) "cultural patrimony" which shall mean an object having ongoing historical, traditional, or cultural importance central to the Native American group or culture itself, rather than property owned by an individual Native

[PUBLIC LAW 101-601--NOV. 16, 1990 104 STAT. 3049]
American, and which, therefore, cannot be alienated, appropriated, or conveyed by any individual regardless of whether or not the individual is a member of the Indian tribe or Native Hawaiian organization and such object shall have been considered inalienable by such Native American group at the time the object was separated from such group.

(4) "Federal agency" means any department, agency, or instrumentality of the United States. Such term does not include the Smithsonian Institution.

(5) "Federal lands" means any land other than tribal lands which are controlled or owned by the United States, including lands selected by but not yet conveyed to Alaska Native Corporations and groups organized pursuant to the Alaska Native Claims Settlement Act of 1971.

(6) "Hui Malama I Na Kupuna O Hawai'i Nei" means the nonprofit, Native Hawaiian organization incorporated under the laws of the State of Hawaii by that name on April 17, 1989, for the purpose of providing guidance and expertise in decisions dealing with Native Hawaiian cultural issues, particularly burial issues.

(7) "Indian tribe" means any tribe, band, nation, or other organized group or community of Indians, including any Alaska Native village (as defined in, or established pursuant to, the Alaska Native Claims Settlement Act), which is recognized as eligible for the special programs and services provided by the United States to Indians because of their status as Indians.

(8) "museum" means any institution or State or local government agency (including any institution of higher learning) that receives Federal funds and has possession of, or control over, Native American cultural items. Such term does not include the Smithsonian Institution or any other Federal agency.

(9) "Native American" means of, or relating to, a tribe, people, or culture that is indigenous to the United States.

(10) "Native Hawaiian" means any individual who is a descendant of the aboriginal people who, prior to 1778, occupied and exercised sovereignty in the area that now constitutes the State of Hawaii.

(11) "Native Hawaiian organization" means any organization which--

(A) serves and represents the interests of Native Hawaiians,

(B) has as a primary and stated purpose the provision of services to Native Hawaiians, and

(C) has expertise in Native Hawaiian Affairs, and shall include the Office of Hawaiian Affairs and Hui Malama I Na Kupuna O Hawai'i Nei.

(12) "Office of Hawaiian Affairs" means the Office of Hawaiian Affairs established by the constitution of the State of Hawaii.

(13) "right of possession" means possession obtained with the voluntary consent of an individual or group that had authority of alienation. The original acquisition of a Native American unassociated funerary object, sacred object or object of cultural patrimony from an Indian tribe or Native Hawaiian organization with the voluntary consent of an individual or group with authority to alienate such object is deemed to give right of possession of that object, unless the phrase so defined would, as

[104 STAT. 3050 PUBLIC LAW 101-601--NOV. 16, 1990]

applied in section 7(c), result in a Fifth Amendment taking by the United States as determined by the United States Claims Court pursuant to 28 U.S.C. 1491 in which event the "right of possession" shall be as provided under otherwise applicable property law. The original acquisition of Native American human remains and

associated funerary objects which were excavated, exhumed, or otherwise obtained with full knowledge and consent of the next of kin or the official governing body of the appropriate culturally affiliated Indian tribe or Native Hawaiian organization is deemed to give right of possession to those remains.

(14) "Secretary" means the Secretary of the Interior.

(15) "tribal land" means-

(A) all lands within the exterior boundaries of any Indian reservation;

(B) all dependent Indian communities;

(C) any lands administered for the benefit of Native Hawaiians pursuant to the Hawaiian Homes Commission Act, 1920, and section 4 of Public Law 86-3.

25 USC 3002.

SEC 3. OWNERSHIP.

(a) NATIVE AMERICAN HUMAN REMAINS AND OBJECTS.—The ownership or control of Native American cultural items which are excavated or discovered on Federal or tribal lands after the date of enactment of this Act shall be (with priority given in the order listed)-

(1) in the case of Native American human remains and associated funerary objects, in the lineal descendants of the Native American; or

(2) in any case in which such lineal descendants cannot be ascertained, and in the case of unassociated funerary objects, sacred objects, and objects of cultural patrimony--

(A) in the Indian tribe or Native Hawaiian organization on whose tribal land such objects or remains were discovered;

Claims.

(B) in the Indian tribe or Native Hawaiian organization which has the closest cultural affiliation with such remains or objects and which, upon notice, states a claim for such remains or objects; or

(C) if the cultural affiliation of the objects cannot be reasonably ascertained and if the objects were discovered on Federal land that is recognized by a final judgment of the Indian Claims Commission or the United States Court of Claims as the aboriginal land of some Indian tribe--

(1) in the Indian tribe that is recognized as aboriginally occupying the area in which the objects were discovered, if upon notice, such tribe states a claim for such remains or objects, or

(2) if it can be shown by a preponderance of the evidence that a different tribe has a stronger cultural relationship with the remains or objects than the tribe or organization specified in paragraph

(1), in the Indian tribe that has the strongest demonstrated relationship, if upon notice, such tribe states a claim for such remains or objects.

Regulations.
(b) UNCLAIMED NATIVE AMERICAN HUMAN REMAINS AND OBJECTS.--Native American cultural items not claimed under subsection [PUBLIC LAW 101-601--NOV. 16,-1990 104 STAT. 3051]

(a) shall be disposed of in accordance with regulations promulgated by the Secretary- in consultation with the review committee established under section 8,-Native American groups, representatives of museums and the scientific community.

(c) INTENTIONAL EXCAVATION AND REMOVAL OF NATIVE AMERICAN HUMAN REMAINS AND OBJECTS.--The intentional removal from or excavation of Native American cultural items from Federal or tribal lands for purposes of discovery, study, or removal of such items is permitted only if--

(1) such items are excavated or removed pursuant to a permit issued under section 4 of the Archaeological Resources Protection Act of 1979 (93 Stat. 721; 16 U.S.C. 470aa et seq.) which shall be consistent with this Act;

(2) such items are excavated or removed after consultation with or, in the case of tribal lands, consent of the appropriate (if any) Indian tribe or Native Hawaiian organization;

(3) the ownership and right of control of the disposition of such items shall be as provided in subsections (a) and (b); and

(4) proof of consultation or consent under paragraph (2) is shown.

(d) INADVERTENT DISCOVERY OF NATIVE AMERICAN REMAINS AND OBJECTS.--(1) Any person who knows, or has reason to know, that such person has discovered Native American cultural items on Federal or tribal lands-after the date of enactment of this Act shall notify, in writing, the Secretary of the Department, or head of any other agency or instrumentality of the United States, having primary management authority with respect to Federal lands and the appropriate Indian tribe or Native Hawaiian organization

with respect to tribal lands, if known or readily ascertainable, and, in the case of lands that have been selected by an Alaska Native Corporation or group organized pursuant to the Alaska Native Claims Settlement Act of 1971, the appropriate corporation or group. If the discovery occurred in connection with an activity, including (but not limited to) construction, mining, logging, and agriculture, the person shall cease the activity in the area of the discovery, make a reasonable effort to protect the items discovered before resuming

such activity, and provide notice under this subsection. Following the notification under this subsection, and upon certification by the Secretary of the department or the head of any agency or instrumentality of the United States or the appropriate Indian tribe or Native Hawaiian organization that notification has been received, the

activity may resume after 30 days of such certification.

(2) The disposition of and control over any cultural items excavated or removed under this subsection shall be determined as provided for in this section.

(3) If the Secretary of the Interior consents, the responsibilities (in whole or in part) under paragraphs (1) and (2) of the Secretary of any department (other than the Department of the Interior) or the head of any other agency or instrumentality may be delegated to the

Secretary with respect to any land managed by such other Secretary or agency head.

(e) RELINQUISHMENT.--Nothing in this section shall prevent the governing body of an Indian tribe or Native Hawaiian organization from expressly relinquishing control over any Native American human remains, or title to or control over any funerary object, or sacred object. [104 STAT. 3052 PUBLIC LAW 101-601--NOV. 16, 1990]

SEC. 4. ILLEGAL TRAFFICKING.

(a) ILLEGAL TRAFFICKING.--Chapter 53 of title 18, United States Code, is amended by adding at the end thereof the following new section:

" 1170. Illegal Trafficking in Native American Human 1170. Illegal Trafficking in Native American Human Remains and Cultural Items

"(a) Whoever knowingly sells, purchases, uses for profit, or transports for sale or profit, the human remains of a Native American without the right of possession to those remains as provided in the Native American Graves Protection and Repatriation Act shall be fined in accordance with this title, or imprisoned not more than 12 months, or both, and in the case of a second or subsequent violation, be fined in accordance with this title, or imprisoned not more than 5 years, or both.

"(b) Whoever knowingly sells, purchases, uses for profit, or transports for sale or profit any Native American cultural items obtained in violation of the Native American Grave Protection and Repatriation Act shall be fined in accordance with this title, imprisoned not more than one year, or both, and in the case of a second or subsequent violation, be fined in accordance with this title, imprisoned not more than 5 years, or both.".

(b) TABLE OF CONTENTS.--The table of contents for chapter 53 of title 18, United States Code, is amended by adding at the end thereof the following new item:

"1170. Illegal Trafficking in Native American Human Remains and Cultural Items.".

Museums.
25 USC 3003.

SEC. 5. INVENTORY FOR HUMAN REMAINS AND ASSOCIATED FUNERARY OBJECTS.

(a) IN GENERAL.--Each Federal agency and each museum which has possession or control over holdings or collections of Native American human remains and associated funerary objects shall compile an inventory of such items and, to the extent possible based on information possessed by such museum or Federal agency, identify the geographical and cultural affiliation of such item.

(b) REQUIREMENTS.--(1) The inventories and identifications required under subsection (a) shall be--

(A) completed in consultation with tribal government and Native Hawaiian organization officials and traditional religious leaders;

(B) completed by not later than the date that is 5 years after the date of enactment of this Act, and

(C) made available both during the time they are being conducted and afterward to a review committee established under section 8.

(2) Upon request by an Indian tribe or Native Hawaiian organization which receives or should have received notice, a museum or Federal agency shall supply additional available documentation to supplement the information required by subsection (a) of this section. The term "documentation" means a summary of existing museum or Federal agency records, including inventories or catalogues, relevant studies, or other pertinent data for the limited purpose of determining the geographical origin, cultural affiliation, and basic facts surrounding acquisition and accession of Native American human remains and associated funerary objects subject to this section. Such term does not mean, and this Act shall not be

[PUBLIC LAW 101-601--NOV. 16, 1990 104 STAT. 3053]

construed to be an authorization for, the initiation of new scientific studies of such remains and associated funerary objects or other means of acquiring or preserving additional scientific information from such remains and objects.

(c) EXTENSION OF TIME FOR INVENTORY.--Any museum which has made a good faith effort to carry out an inventory and identification under this section, but which has been unable to complete the process, may appeal to the Secretary for an extension of the time requirements set forth in subsection (b)(1)(B). The Secretary may extend such time requirements for any such museum upon a finding of good faith effort. An indication of good faith shall include the development of a plan to carry out the inventory and identification process.

(d) NOTIFICATION--(1) If the cultural affiliation of any particular Native American human remains or associated funerary objects is determined pursuant to this section, the Federal agency or museum concerned shall, not later than 6 months after the completion of the inventory, notify the affected Indian tribes or Native Hawaiian organizations.

(2) The notice required by paragraph (1) shall include information--

(A) which identifies each Native American human remains or associated funerary objects and the circumstances surrounding its acquisition;

(B) which lists the human remains or associated funerary objects that are clearly identifiable as to tribal origin; and (C) which lists the Native American human remains and associated funerary objects that are not clearly identifiable as being culturally affiliated with that Indian tribe or Native Hawaiian organization, but which, given the totality of circumstances surrounding acquisition of the remains or objects, are determined by a reasonable belief to be remains or objects culturally affiliated with the Indian tribe or Native Hawaiian organization.

Federal
Register,
publication

(3) A copy of each notice provided under paragraph (1) shall be sent to the Secretary who shall publish each notice in the Federal Register.
(e) INVENTORY.--For the purposes of this section, the term "inventory" means a simple itemized list that summarizes the information called for by this section.

25 USC 3004.

SEC. 6. SUMMARY FOR UNASSOCIATED FUNERARY OBJECTS, SACRED OBJECTS, AND CULTURAL PATRIMONY.

Museums.

(a) IN GENERAL.--Each Federal agency or museum which has possession or control over holdings or collections of Native American unassociated funerary objects, sacred objects, or objects of cultural patrimony shall provide a written summary of such objects based upon available information held by such agency or museum. The summary shall describe the scope of the collection, kinds of objects included, reference to geographical location, means and period of acquisition and cultural affiliation, where readily ascertainable.
(b) REQUIREMENTS.-- (1) The summary required under subsection (a) shall be--
(A) in lieu of an object-by-object inventory;
(B) followed by consultation with tribal government and Native Hawaiian organization officials and traditional religious leaders; and
[104 STAT. 3054 PUBLIC LAW 101-601--NOV. 16, 1990]
(C) completed by not later than the date that is 3 years after the date of enactment of this Act.
(2) Upon request, Indian Tribes and Native Hawaiian organizations shall have access to records, catalogues, relevant studies or other pertinent data for the limited purposes of determining the geographic origin, cultural affiliation, and basic facts surrounding acquisition and accession of Native American objects subject to this section. Such information shall be provided in a reasonable manner to be agreed upon by all parties.

25 USC 3005.

SEC. 7. REPATRIATION.
(a) REPATRIATION OF NATIVE AMERICAN HUMAN REMAINS AND OBJECTS POSSESSED OR CONTROLLED BY FEDERAL AGENCIES AND MUSEUMS.--
(1) If, pursuant to section 5, the cultural affiliation of Native American human remains and associated funerary objects with a particular Indian tribe or Native Hawaiian organization is established, then the Federal agency or museum, upon the request of a known lineal descendant of the Native American or of the tribe or organization and pursuant to subsections (b) and (e) of this section, shall expeditiously return such remains and associated funerary objects.
(2) If, pursuant to section 6, the cultural affiliation with a particular Indian tribe or Native Hawaiian organization is shown with respect to unassociated funerary objects, sacred objects or objects of cultural patrimony, then the Federal agency or museum, upon the request of the Indian tribe or Native Hawaiian organization and pursuant to subsections (b), (c) and (e) of this section, shall expeditiously return such objects.

(3) The return of cultural items covered by this Act shall be in consultation with the requesting lineal descendant or tribe or organization to determine the place and manner of delivery of such items.

(4) Where cultural affiliation of Native American human remains and funerary objects has not been established in an inventory prepared pursuant to section 5, or the summary pursuant to section 6, or where Native American human remains and funerary objects are not included upon any such inventory, then, upon request and pursuant to subsections (b) and (e) and, in the case of unassociated funerary objects, subsection (c), such Native American human remains and funerary objects shall be expeditiously returned where the requesting Indian tribe or Native Hawaiian organization can show cultural affiliation by a preponderance of the evidence based upon geographical, kinship, biological, archaeological, anthropological, linguistic, folkloric, oral traditional, historical, or other relevant information or expert opinion.

(5) Upon request and pursuant to subsections (b), (c) and (e), sacred objects and objects of cultural patrimony shall be expeditiously returned where--

(A) the requesting party is the direct lineal descendant of an individual who owned the sacred object;

(B) the requesting Indian tribe or Native Hawaiian organization can show that the object was owned or controlled by the tribe or organization; or

(C) the requesting Indian tribe or Native Hawaiian organization can show that the sacred object was owned or controlled by a member thereof, provided that in the case where a sacred object was owned by a member thereof, there are no identifiable

[PUBLIC LAW 101-601--NOV. 16, 1990 104 STAT. 3055]
lineal descendants of said member or the lineal descendent, upon notice, have failed to make a claim for the object under this Act.

(b) SCIENTIFIC STUDY.--If the lineal descendant, Indian tribe, or Native Hawaiian organization requests the return of culturally affiliated Native American cultural items, the Federal agency or museum shall expeditiously return such items unless such items are indispensable for completion of a specific scientific study, the outcome of which would be of major benefit to the United States. Such items shall be returned by no later than 90 days after the
date on which the scientific study is completed.

(c) STANDARD OF REPATRIATION.--If a known lineal descendant or an Indian tribe or Native Hawaiian organization requests the return of Native American unassociated funerary objects, sacred objects or objects of cultural patrimony pursuant to this Act and presents
evidence which, if standing alone before the introduction of evidence to the contrary, would support a finding that the Federal agency or museum did not have the right of possession, then such agency or museum shall return such objects unless it can overcome such inference and prove that it has a right of possession to the objects.

25 USC 3006.   (d) SHARING OF INFORMATION BY FEDERAL AGENCIES AND
MUSEUMS.--Any Federal agency or museum shall share what
information it does possess regarding the object in question with the known
lineal descendant, Indian tribe, or Native Hawaiian organization to assist in
making a claim under this section.

(e) COMPETING CLAIMS.--Where there are multiple requests for
repatriation of any cultural item and, after complying with the requirements
of this Act, the Federal agency or museum cannot clearly determine which
requesting party is the most appropriate claimant, the agency or museum
may retain such item until the requesting parties agree upon its disposition
or the dispute is otherwise resolved pursuant to the provisions of this Act or
by a court of competent jurisdiction.

(f) MUSEUM OBLIGATION.--Any museum which repatriates any
item in good faith pursuant to this Act shall not be liable for claims by an
aggrieved party or for claims of breach of fiduciary duty, public trust, or
violations of state law that are inconsistent with the provisions of this Act.

SEC. 8. REVIEW COMMITTEE.

(a) ESTABLISHMENT.--Within 120 days after the date of enactment of
this Act, the Secretary shall establish a committee to monitor and review the
implementation of the inventory and identification process and repatriation
activities required under sections 5, 6 and 7.

(b) MEMBERSHIP--(1) The Committee established under subsection (a)
shall be composed of 7 members,

(A) 3 of whom shall be appointed by the Secretary from nominations
submitted by Indian tribes, Native Hawaiian organizations, and traditional
Native American religious leaders with at least 2 of such persons being
traditional Indian religious leaders;

(B) 3 of whom shall be appointed by the Secretary from nominations
submitted by national museum organizations and scientific organizations;
and

(C) 1 who shall be appointed by the Secretary from a list of persons
developed and consented to by all of the members appointed pursuant to
subparagraphs (A) and (B).

[104 STAT 3056 PUBLIC LAW 101-601--NOV. 16, 1990]

(2) The Secretary may not appoint Federal officers or employees to the
committee.

(3) In the event vacancies shall occur, such vacancies shall be filled by the
Secretary in the same manner as the original appointment within 90 days of
the occurrence of such vacancy.

(4) Members of the committee established under subsection (a) shall serve
without pay, but shall be reimbursed at a rate equal to the daily rate for GS-
18 of the General Schedule for each day (including travel time) for which
the member is actually engaged in committee business. Each member shall
receive travel expenses, including per diem in lieu of subsistence, in
accordance with sections 5702 and 5703 of title 5, United States Code.

Regulations.   (c) RESPONSIBILITIES.--The committee established under subsection a)
shall be responsible for-

(1) designating one of the members of the committee as chairman;

(2) monitoring the inventory and identification process conducted under
sections 5 and 6 to ensure a fair, objective consideration and assessment of
all available relevant information and evidence;

(3) upon the request of any affected party, reviewing and making findings
related to-

(A) the identity or cultural affiliation of cultural items, or

(B) the return of such items;

(4) facilitating the resolution of any disputes among Indian tribes, Native
Hawaiian organizations, or lineal descendants and Federal agencies or
museums relating to the return of such items including convening the parties
to the dispute if deemed desirable;

(5) compiling an inventory of culturally unidentifiable human remains that
are in the possession or control of each Federal agency and museum and
recommending specific actions for developing a process for disposition of
such remains;

(6) consulting with Indian tribes and Native Hawaiian organizations and
museums on matters within the scope of the work of the committee
affecting such tribes or organizations;

(7) consulting with the Secretary in the development of regulations to carry
out this Act;

(8) performing such other related functions as the Secretary -may assign to
the committee; and

(9) making recommendations, if appropriate, regarding future care of
cultural items which are to be repatriated.

(d) Any records and findings made by the review committee pursuant to this
Act relating to the identity or cultural affiliation of any cultural items and
the return of such items may be admissible in any action brought under
section 15 of this Act.

(e) RECOMMENDATIONS AND REPORT.--The committee shall make
the recommendations under paragraph (c)(5) in consultation
with Indian tribes and Native Hawaiian organizations and appropriate
scientific and museum groups.

(f) ACCESS.--The Secretary shall ensure that the committee established
under subsection (a) and the members of the committee have reasonable
access to Native American cultural items under review and to associated
scientific and historical documents.

(g) DUTIES OF SECRETARY.--The Secretary shall—

(1) establish such rules and regulations for the committee as may be
necessary, and

[PUBLIC LAW 101-601--NOV 16, 1990 104 STAT. 3057]

(2) provide reasonable administrative and staff support necessary for the
deliberations of the committee.

(h) ANNUAL REPORT.--The committee established under subsection (a) shall submit an annual report to the Congress on the progress made, and any barriers encountered, in implementing this section during the previous year.

(i) TERMINATION.--The committee established under subsection (a) shall terminate at the end of the 120-day period beginning on the day the Secretary certifies, in a report submitted to Congress, that the work of the committee has been completed.

Museums.

25 USC 3007.

SEC. 9. PENALTY.

(a) PENALTY.--Any museum that fails to comply with the requirements of this Act may be assessed a civil penalty by the Secretary of the Interior pursuant to procedures established by the Secretary through regulation. A penalty assessed under this subsection shall be determined on the record after opportunity for an agency hearing. Each violation under this subsection shall be a separate offense.

(b) AMOUNT OF PENALTY.--The amount of a penalty assessed under subsection (a) shall be determined under regulations promulgated pursuant to this Act, taking into account, in addition to other factors--

(1) the archaeological, historical, or commercial value of the item involved;

(2) the damages suffered, both economic and noneconomic, by an aggrieved party, and

(3) the number of violations that have occurred.

(c) ACTIONS TO RECOVER PENALTIES.--If any museum fails to pay courts. an assessment of a civil penalty pursuant

Courts.

to a final order of the Secretary that has been issued under subsection (a) and not appealed or after a final judgment has been rendered on appeal of such order, the Attorney General may institute a civil action in an appropriate district court of the United States to collect the penalty. In such action, the validity and amount of such penalty shall not be subject to review.

(d) SUBPOENAS.--In hearings held pursuant to subsection (a), subpoenas may be issued for the attendance and testimony of witnesses and the production of relevant papers, books, and documents. Witnesses so summoned shall be paid the same fees and mileage that are paid to witnesses in the courts of the United States.

25 USC 3008.

SEC. 10. GRANTS.

(a) INDIAN TRIBES AND NATIVE HAWAIIAN ORGANIZATIONS.-- The Secretary is authorized to make grants to Indian tribes and Native Hawaiian organizations for the purpose of assisting such tribes and organizations in the repatriation of Native American cultural items.

(b) MUSEUMS.--The Secretary is authorized to make grants to museums for the purpose of assisting the museums in conducting the inventories and identification required under sections 5 and 6.

25 USC 3009.   SEC. 11. SAVINGS PROVISIONS.
Nothing in this Act shall be construed to--
(1) limit the authority of any Federal agency or museum to--
(A) return or repatriate Native American cultural items to Indian tribes,
Native Hawaiian organizations, or individuals, and
[104 STAT. 3058 PUBLIC LAW 101--601--NOV. 16, 1990]
(B) enter into any other agreement with the consent of the culturally
affiliated tribe or organization as to the disposition of, or control over, items
covered by this Act;
(2) delay actions on repatriation requests that are pending on the date of
enactment of this Act;
(3) deny or otherwise affect access to any court;
(4) limit any procedural or substantive right which may otherwise be
secured to individuals or Indian tribes or Native Hawaiian organizations; or
(5) limit the application of any State or Federal law pertaining to theft or
stolen property.

25 USC 3010.   SEC. 12. SPECIAL RELATIONSHIP BETWEEN FEDERAL
GOVERNMENT AND INDIAN TRIBES.
This Act reflects the unique relationship between the Federal Government
and Indian tribes and Native Hawaiian organizations and should not be
construed to establish a precedent with respect to any other individual,
organization or foreign government.

25 USC 3011.   SEC. 13. REGULATIONS.
The Secretary shall promulgate regulations to carry out this Act within 12
months of enactment.

25 USC 3012.   SEC. 14. AUTHORIZATION OF APPROPRIATIONS.
There is authorized to be appropriated such sums as may be necessary to
carry out this Act.

25 USC 3013.   SEC. 15. ENFORCEMENT.
The United States district courts shall have jurisdiction over any action
brought by any person alleging a violation
Courts.   of this Act and shall have the authority to issue such orders as may be
necessary to enforce the provisions of this Act.

REFERENCES

Alderfer JD. 2006. Connections and Expressions of Faith Cheyenne, Arapaho, Mennonite: Journey from Darlington, Oklahoma. *MHEP Quarterly* 9(2):2-4.

American Association of Physical Anthropologists. (2000). Statement by the American Association of Physical Anthropologists on the Secretary of the Interior's Letter of 21 September 2000 Regarding Cultural Affiliation of Kennewick Man. http://www.physanth.org.

Aromäki RE, Lindman, CJP. 1999. Testosterone, aggressiveness, and antisocial personality. *Aggressive Behavior* 25: 113-123.

Ayau EH. (Hui Malama I Na Kupuna O Hawai'I Nei, Hale'iwa, HI. huimalam@@pixi.com). Rooted in Native Soil [Internet]. Hale'iwa (HI): Hui Malama I Na Kupuna O Hawai'I I Nei; [cited 2007 Jul 12]. 4 p. Available from: http://huimalama.tripod.com/rooted.htm.

Balter M. 2000. Archaeologists and Rabbis Clash Over Human Remains. *Science* 287(5450):34-35.

Baker BJ, Varney TL, Wilkinson RG, Anderson LM, Liston MA. 2001. Repatriation and the Study of Human Remains. In: Bray TL editor. *The Future of the Past: Archaeologists, Native Americans, and Repatriation*. New York: Garland Publishing. p 69-90.

Bancroft R. Everything Relates, or a Holistic Approach to Aboriginal Indigenous Cultural Heritage [Internet]. Canberra (Australia): Australian National University; [cited 2007 Jul 24]. 4 p. Available from: http://www.folklife.si.edu/resources/Unesco/bancroft.htm.

Bell L, Wilson A. 2002. Haida First Nations repatriate human remains from USA [internet]. New York (NY): Indian Burial and Sacred Ground Watch; [cited 2007 Jul 12]. 2 p. Available from: http://www.ibsgwatch.imagedjinn.com/learn/202sept12haida.htm.

Bender P. 2004. Testimony Before the United States Senate Committee on Indian Affairs.

Bethune B, MacQueen K. 2001. Bones of Contention. *Maclean's* 114(12):30.

Bird J. 2000. Cultural Resources & Historic Preservation "Message From the Eastern Band of Cherokee" [Internet]. Cherokee News Path; [cited 2007 Jul 12]. 3 p. Available from: http://www.yvwiiusdinvnohii.net/Cherokee/News2000/Feb2000/EBCI000226Bird.htm.

Bray TL. 1996. Repatriation, power relations and the politics of the past. *Antiquity* 70(268): 440-445.

Bray TL. 2001. *The future of the past: Archaeologists, Native Americans, and repatriation*. New York: Garland Publishing.

Boswell, R. 2002. Bones of Contention: The Museum of Civilization is Set to Return Dozens of Ancestral Bones to Area Native People, but the Algonquins Want More. *The Ottawa Citizen*. A1.

Brothwell D. 2004. Bring out your dead: people, pots and politics. *Antiquity* 78: 414-418.

Brown MF, Bruchac MM. 2006. NAGPRA from the middle distance: Legal puzzles and unintended consequences. In: Merryman JH editor. *Imperialism, Art, and Restitution*. New York: Cambridge University Press. p. 193-217.

Brundin JA. 1996. A New Cultural Agenda for the National Museum of the Americana Indian. Academic Questions. *Fall*: 35-43.

Bruning SB. 2006. Complex Legal Legacies: The Native American Graves Protection and Repatriation Act, Scientific Study, and Kennewick Man. *American Antiquity* 71(3):501-521.

Buikstra JE, Ubelaker, DH. 1994. *Standards: For Data Collections From Human Skeletal Remains*. Fayetteville, AR: Arkansas Archaeological Survey.

Chatters JC. 1997. Encounter with an ancestor. *Anthropology Newsletter* 38(1): 9-10.

Clark GA. 1998. NAGPRA, the conflict between science and religion, and the political consequences. Society for American Archaeology Bulletin 16(5). Available from: http://www.saa.org/publications/saabulletin/16-5/Society for American Archaeology16.html.

Clark GA. 1999. NAGPRA, science, and the demon-haunted world (Native American Graves Protection and Repatriation Act). Skeptical Inquirer May-June 1999:44-49.

Cole D. 1985. Captured heritage: The scramble for Northwest coast artifacts. Tulsa: University of Oklahoma Press.

Connolly J. 2006. Feb 19. NAGPRA [personal e-mail]. Accessed 2006 Feb 19.

Crambilt A. 2006. Feb 16. Impediment to Science? [personal e-mail]. Accessed 2006 Feb 16.

Crelier M. 2006. Feb 20. From Taos Pueblo Tribal Court [personal e-mail]. Accessed 2006 Feb 20.

Cubillo F. 2003. Give it back you bastards: Indigenous perspectives on the repatriation of human remains, Repatriation for a New Century. World Archaeological Congress, Washington DC, USA.

Custred G. 2001. Oral traditions and rules of evidence. Mammoth Trumpet. 16: 1.

Daily M. 2007. Scientists protest tribal control over ancient remains. Associated Press. Washington D.C. December 7th.

Dansie A. 1999. International implications of the impact of repatriation in Nevada museums. Society for American Archaeology Bulletin 17(3). Available from: http://www.saa.org/publications/saabulletin/17-3/saa14.html.

Dansie A, Tuohy D. 1997. What we can and can't know about Great Basin prehistory. *Anthropology Newsletter* 38(1): 11.

Dawkins R. 2006. *The God delusion*. London: Houghton Mifflin.

Dongoske KE. 2000. NAGPRA: A New Beginning, Not the End, for Osteological Analysis – A Hopi Perspective. In: Mihesuah DA. *Repatriation Reader: Who Owns American Indian Remains?* Lincoln: University of Nebraska Press. p 282-293.

Echo-Hawk W. [2006]. NAGPRA/Legislative Issues Case Update. Native American Rights Fund; [cited 2007 Jul 12]. 1 p. Available from: http://www.narf.org/cases/nagpra.html.

Erickson J. 2006. Ancient Puebloans reburied at park [Internet]. Denver (CO): Rocky Mountain News; [cited 2007 Jul 12]. 2 p. Available from:

http://www.rockymountainnews.com/drmn/local/article/0,1299,DRMN_15_4674745,00. html.

Fforde C. 2004. *Collecting the Dead: Archaeology and the reburial issue*. London: Duckworth Publisher.

Fine-Dare K. 2002. *Grave Injustice: The American Indian repatriation movement and NAGPRA*. Lincoln: University of Nebraska Press.

Foley H. 2006 Feb 17. *NAGPRA vs. Interests of Science* [personal e-mail]. Accessed 2006 Feb 17.

Garza CE, Powell S. 2001. Ethics and the Past: Reburial and Repatriation in American Archaeology. In: Bray TL editor. *The Future of the Past: Archaeologists, Native Americans, and Repatriation*. New York: Garland Publishing. p. 37-56.

Gibbon KF editor. 2005. *Who Owns the Past?* New Brunswick (NJ): Rutgers University Press.

Green G. 2006. Mennonites Plan Big Meeting Here [Internet]. Clinton: Clinton Daily News Archives and Search; [cited 2007 Jul 27]. 3 p. Available from: http://www.clintondailynews.com/cgi-bin/newspost/extras/archives.cgi?category=2&view=1.07.0.

Grimes RL. 2001. Desecration: An Interreligious Controversy. In: Bray TL editor. *The Future of the Past: Archaeologists, Native Americans*, and Repatriation. New York: Garland Publishing. p. 91-106.

Hall DA, Wisner G. 2000. Public Policy: Many Concerns, Few Answers [Internet]. Center for the Study of the First Americans; [cited 2007 Aug 15]. 6 p. Available from: http://www.centerfirstamericans.org/mt.php?a=4.

Hall TG. 1999. Testimony of Tex G. Hall, Chairman. Submitted to the Senate Committee on Indian Affairs.

Harjo SS. 2007. Realistic New Year's resolution for others. *Indian Country Today* 26(30):A3.

Hawkinson C., Walton B. 2001. *Evidence of the Past: A Map and Status of Ancient Remains* [internet]. *Friends of America's Past*; [cited 2007 Aug 29]. 6 p. Available from: http://www.friendsofpast.org/earliest-americans/map.html.

Hemming S. Ngarrindjeri Burials as Cultural Sites: Indigenous Heritage Issues in Australia [Internet]. Australia: World Archaeological Congress; [modified 2007 Jul; cited 2007 Jul 23]. 5 p. Available from: http://www.worldarchaeologicalcongress.org/site/bulletin/wab11/hemming.php.

Henderson K. 2006 Feb 17. *NAGPRA Impedes Science?* [personal e-mail]. Accessed 2006 Feb 17.

Horn J. 2006 Feb 17. Native Graves [personal e-mail]. Accessed 2006 Feb 17. Human Remains and Ethnographic Summaries [internet]. Albany (NY): University at Albany; [cited 2007 Jul 12]. 3 p. Available from: http://www.albany.edu/kj1528/isp523/finalproject/native.html

Hunt M. 1999. *The new Know-Nothings: The Political Foes of the Scientific Study of Human Nature*. New Brunswick: Transaction.

Johnson G. 1996. *Indian Tribes' Creationists Thwart Archeologists*. The New York Times. Available from: http://www.santafe.edu/~johnson/articles.creation.html.

Josephson ES. 2006 Feb 17. NAGPRA [personal e-mail]. Accessed 2006 Feb 17.

Klesert AL, Powell S. 1993. A perspective on ethics and the reburial controversy. *American Antiquity* 58(2):348-355.

Kluger J, Cray D. 2006. Who Should Own the Bones? *Time* 167(11):50-51

Lange J. 1997. Native Americans reclaim sacred objects [Internet]. Seattle (WA): University of Washington; [cited 2007 Jul 12]. 5 p. Available from: http://archives.thedaily.washington.edu/1997/031397/repat.031397.html.

Larsen CS. 2003. *Bioarchaeology: interpreting behavior from the human skeleton.* Cambridge: Cambridge University Press.

Larsen CS, Walker PL. 2006. The Ethics of Bioarchaeology. In: Turner TR editor. *Biological Anthropology and Ethics: From Repatriation to Genetic Identity.* 2nd Edition. New York: State University of New York Press. p. 111-121.

Lepper BT. 2003. Kennewick Man ruling defended in US Court of Appeals. *American Association of Physical Anthropologists Newsletter* 4(3): 1-4.

Lewin S. 2006. NAGPRA and scientists. *Native American Times* 7(9):2

Lightfoot KG. 2006. Collaboration: *The Future of the Study of the Past. News From Native California* 19(2):28.

Lovell NC. 1991. An evolutionary framework for assessing illness and injury in nonhuman primates. *American Journal of Physical Anthropology* 34S: 117-155.

MacKinnon M. 2000. Haida remains sent back to B. C. for second burial. *The Globe and Mail*: A5.

Maines S. 2006. KU hopes to return a dozen artifacts to tribes within months [Internet]. Kansas City: Journal World; [cited 2007 Jul 12]. 2 p. Available from: http://www2.ljworld.com/news/2006/aug/10/ku_hopes_return_dozen_artifacts_tribes_within_mont/.

Martinez III MD. 2006 Feb 16. *Sacred Sites Stay Sacred* [personal e-mail]. Accessed 2006 Feb 16.

Meighan CW. 1993. Burying American Archaeology [Internet]. Friends of America's Past; [cited 2007 Jul 23]. 4 p. Available from http://www.friendsofpast.org/forum/burying.html.

Meighan CW. 1999. Burying American Archaeology [internet]. Archaeology; [cited 2007 Jul 23]. 4 p. Available from: http://www.archaeology.org/online/features/native/debate.html.

Meighan CW. 2000. Some Scholars' View on Reburial. In: Mihesuah DA. Repatriation Reader: Who Owns American Indian Remains? Lincoln: University of Nebraska Press. p. 190-199.

McKeown CT, Hutt S. 2003. In the smaller scope of conscience: the Native American Graves and Protection and Repatriation Act twelve years after. University of California, LA *Journal of Environmental Law and Policy* 21: 153-154.

Merbs CF. 1996. Spondylolysis and spondylolisthesis: A cost of being an erect biped or a clever adaptation. *Yearbook of Physical Anthropology* 39: 201-228.

Mihesuah D. ed. 2000. Repatriation Reader: Who Owns American Indian Remains? Lincoln: University of Nebraska Press.

Minthorn A. [date unknown]. Testimony of Armand Minthorn for the Confederated Tribes of the Umatilla Indian Reservation.

Morris J. 2006. Comments on Weiss. *The Society for American Archaeology Archaeological Record* (Sept. 2006):4.

Muska DD. [1998] Scalping Science: Sensitivity Run Amok May Silence the Spirit Cave Mummy Forever [Internet]. Nevada: Nevada Journal; [cited 2007 Aug 29]. 10 p. Available from: http://nj.npri.org/nj98/02/cover_story.htm. National Park Service. [2004]. International Repatriation [Internet]. US Department of the Interior; [cited 2007

Jul 23]. 8 p. Available from: http://www.nps.gov/history/Nagpra/SPECIAL/ International.htm.

Nattero R. 2006. The Declarations at the United Nations: Working Group on Indigenous Populations [internet]. Geneva: Ecospirituality Foundation; cited 2007 Jul 24]. 4 p. Available from: http://www.eco-spirituality.org/au-wwe8.htm.

O'Hagan M. 1998. Bones of contention: The agendas that have brought a 9,300-year old skeleton to life. Willamette Week. Available from: http://wweek.com/ ALL_OLD_HTML/cover042298.html

Ousley SD, WT Bileck, RE Hollinger. 2005. *Federal repatriation legislation and the role of physical anthropology in repatriation*. 128: 2- 32.

Paddock R. 2008. *American Indians want to rebury remains dug up by Berkeley archaeologists*. Los Angeles Times. January 13. Pang GYK. 2006. Dispute delivers praise and scorn to Hui Malama [Internet]. Honolulu (HI): The Honolulu Advertiser; [cited 2007 Jul12]. 5 p. Available from: http://the.honoluluadvertiser.com/article/2006/Jan/13/In/FP601130347.html

Politis G. 2001. On archaeology praxis, gender bias and indigenous peoples in South America. *Journal of Social Archaeology* 1:90-107.

Preston D. 1997. The lost man. *The New Yorker*: 70-78, 80-81.

Ratnawati N. 2007. *Repatriation: Contemporary Relationships Between Archaeologists and Indians in California* [dissertation]. San Francisco (CA): San Francisco State University. 164 p.

Reinhard KJ, Tieszen L, Sandness KL, Beiningen LM, Miller E, Ghazi A, Miewalk CD, Barnum SV. 1994. Trade, contact, and female health in northeast Nebraska. In: Larsen CS, Milner GJ, editors. *In the wake of contact: Biological responses to conquest*. New York: Wiley-Liss. p. 63-74.

Reynolds J. 2007. Washington in Brief. Indian Country Today 26(47):A4.

Riding In J. 2000. Repatriation: A Pawnee's Perspective. In: Mihesuah DA. *Repatriation Reader: Who Owns American Indian Remains?* Lincoln: University of Nebraska Press. p. 106-122.

Roberts CA, JE Buikstra. 2003. *The Bioarchaeology of Tuberculosis: A Global View on a Reemerging Disease*. Gainesville: University Press of Florida.

Rose JC, Green TJ, Green VD. 1996. NAGPRA is Forever. *Annual Review of Anthropology* 25:81-103.

Rothschild BM, Fernando LC, Coppa A, Rothschild C. 2000. First European Exposure to Syphilis: The Dominican Republic at the Time of Columbian Contact. *Clinical Infectious Diseases*. 31: 936-941.

Rothstein E. 2006. Protection for Indian Patrimony That Leads to a Paradox [Internet]. New York: New York Times; [cited 2007 Jul 12]. 4 p. Available from: http://www.williams.edu/go/native/paradoxes.htm.

Schneider AL. 2001. What is the Meaning of Native American [Internet]? [place unknown]: Center for the Study of the First Americans; [cited 2007 Jul 12]. 4 p. Available from: http://www.centerfirstamericans.com/mt.php?a=15.

Seidemann RM. 2003. Time For A Change? The Kennewick Man Case And Its Implications For The Future Of The Native American Graves Protection And Repatriation Act. Morgantown (WV): *West Virginia Law Review* 149-176.

Seidemann RM. 2003. Congressional Intent: What Is the Purpose of NAGPRA? *Mammoth Trumpet* 18(3):1-2, 19-20.

Seidemann RM. 2004. Bones of Contention: A Comparative Examination of Law Governing Human Remains from Archaeological Contexts in Formerly Colonial Countries. Baton Rouge (LA): *Louisiana Law Review* 64(3):1-38.

Seidemann RM. 2004. The Other Front of the War: Legislative Attempts to Alter NAGPRA. *Mammoth Trumpet* 19(3):1, 19-20.

Seidemann RM. 2004. What Is the Significance of "Is"? Another Attempt to Amend NAGPRA. Mammoth Trumpet, *Center for the Study of the First Americans* 20(1):1, 14-15.

Sharpe K, Fawbert H. 1998. Whose Heritage? The Conflict between Living and the Dead within Archaeology [Internet]. Science and Spirit; [cited 2007 Jul 24]. 4 p. Available from: http://www.science-spirit.org/printerfriendly.php?article_id=22.

Springer JW. 2005. Scholarship vs. Repatriation. Academic Questions. Winter:6-36.

Stapp D. 2006. Tribal involvement enriches Mid-Columbia archaeology [Internet]. Pasco (WA): Tri-City Herald; [cited 2007 Sep 28]. 2 p. Available from: http://proquest.umi.com/pqdweb?index=15&sid=6&srchmode=1&vinst=PROD&fmt=3& startpag.

Thomas DH. 2001. Skull wars: Kennewick Man, archaeology, and the battle for Native American identity. New York: Basic Books.

Thomas L. 2004. Nov 7. *Ancient Indian remains raise complex issues*. Pittsburgh Post-Gazette.

Thomas R. 2006 Feb 18. supporting NAPGRA [personal e-mail]. Accessed 2006 Feb 18.

Trope JF, Echo-Hawk WR. 2001. The Native American Graves Protection and Repatriation Act: Background and Legislative History. In: Bray TL editor. The Future of the Past: Archaeologists, Native Americans, and Repatriation. New York: Garland Publishing. p. 9-36.

Truscott MC. 2006. *Repatriation of Indigenous cultural property*. Paper prepared for 2006 Australian State of the Environment Committee, Department of the Environment and Heritage; Canberra (Australia).

Tsosie R. 2000 The Native American Graves Protection and Repatriation Act: Testimony of Rebecca Tsosie. United States Senate Committee on Indian Affairs Oversight Hearing.

Ubelaker DH, Grant LG. 1989. Human skeletal remains: preservation or reburial? *Yearbook of Physical Anthropology* 32: 249-287.

Vincent S. 2004. Grave Injustice [Internet]. Reason Online; [cited 2007 Jun 6]. 6 p. Available from: http://www.reason.com/news/printer/29202.html.

Walker PL. 1997. Wife beating, boxing, and broken noses: Skeletal evidence for the cultural patterning of violence, in: D.L. Martin, D.W. Frayer, editors. In: *Troubled Times: Violence and warfare in the past*. Gordon and Breach Publishers, Amsterdam. p.145-179.

Walker PL. 2001. An Appeal from Israel [internet]. *Friends of America's Past*; [cited 2007 Jul 23]. 4 p. Available from: http://www.friendsofpast.org/earliest-americans/israel.html

Wallis RJ, Blain J. 2001. A British Reburial Issue [Internet]? Southampton (UK): *Centre for Research on Human Rights*; [modified 2002 Jan 10; cited 2007 Jul 20]. 8 p. Available from: http://www.sacredsites.org.uk/reports/reburial.html.

Watkins J. 2000. Tribalizing Public Archaeology [Internet]. American Anthropological Association; [cited 2007 Jul 24]. 6 p. Available from: http://p-j.net/pjeppson/AAA2000/Papers/Watkins.htm.

Watzman H. 1996. Israel's Reburial Debate [Internet]. Archaeological Institute of America; [cited 2007 Jul23]. 1 p. Available from: http://www.archaeology.org/9609/newsbriefs/israel.html.

Weiss E. 1998. Sexual differences in activity patterns of a Central Californian hunter-gatherer population. *California Anthropologist* 25: 1-7.

Weiss E. 2001. Kennewick Man's Funeral: The Burying of Scientific Evidence. *Politics and the Life Sciences* 20(1):13-18.

Weiss E. 2001. Cross-cultural study of humeri: Environmental causes of morphology. Unpublished doctoral dissertation, University of Arkansas, Fayetteville.

Weiss E. 2001. Kennewick Man's behavior: a CT scan analysis. *American Journal of Physical Anthropology Supplement* 32: 163 (Abstract).

Weiss E. 2002. Drought-related changes in two hunter-gatherer California populations. *Quaternary Research* 58: 393-396.

Weiss E. 2003. Understanding muscle markers: Aggregation and construct validity. *American Journal of Physical Anthropology* 121: 230-240.

Weiss E. 2003. Humeral cross-sections and the physical environment. *American Journal of Physical Anthropology* 121: 293-302.

Weiss E. 2004. Understanding muscle markers: Lower limbs. *American Journal of Physical Anthropology* 125: 232-238.

Weiss E. 2005. Humeral cross-sectional morphology from 18th-century Quebec prisoners of war: Limits to activity reconstruction. *American Journal of Physical Anthropology* 126: 311-317.

Weiss E. 2005. Understanding osteoarthritis patterns: An examination of aggregate osteoarthritis. *Journal of Paleopathology* 16: 87-98.

Weiss E. 2005 Schmorl's nodes: A preliminary investigation. *Paleopathology Newsletter* 132: 6-10.

Weiss E. 2006. Osteoarthritis and body mass. *Journal of Archaeological Science* 33: 690-695.

Weiss E. 2006. NAGPRA: Before and after. Friends of America's Past. http://www.friendsofpast.org/nagpra/06WeissNAGPRA.pdf.

Weiss E. 2006. Research and NAGPRA. *Society for American Archaeology Archaeological Record* 6: 29-31.

Weiss E. 2006. *Research and NAGPRA*. ACPAC Newsletter. September Issue: 1-2.

Weiss E. 2007. Muscle Markers Revisited: Activity pattern reconstructed with controls in a central California Amerind Population. *American Journal of Physical Anthropology* 133: 931-940.

Weiss E. in press. Facial trauma in a prehistoric California population: patterns and comparisons. *Journal of Paleopathology*.

Weiss E, Jurmain RD 2007. In and out of joint: Osteoarthritis revisited. *International Journal of Osteoarchaeology* 17: 437-450.

Whettstone DM. 2005. What the Land Might Tell Us. MCC Washington Memo July-August 2005:3.

Wilson J. 2003. He Straddles 2 Worlds to Rebury Ancestors – Reinterring bones exposed by bulldozers is vital, tribal officials say. He only smoothes way for developers, critics insist

[Internet]. National Association of Tribal Historic Preservation Officers; [cited 2007 Jul12]. 3 p. Available from: http://www.nathpo.org/News/NAGPRA/News-NAGPRA26.htm.

Zimmerman LJ. 2001. Usurping Native American Voice. In: Bray TL editor. The Future of the Past: Archaeologists, Native Americans, and Repatriation. New York: Garland Publishing. p. 169-184.

Author Unknown. 1995. Confession of Faith in a Mennonite Perspective, 1995 [internet]. Mennonite Church USA; [cited 2007 Jul 27]. 2 p. Available from: http://www.mcusa-archives.ord/library/resolutions/1995/1995-5.html.

Author Unknown. 1997. Public disquiet over digging of graves. *British Archaeology*. 29: 5.

Author Unknown. 1998. Coalition Wants Ouster of UNL Professor. Ojibwe News Dec. 4 .

Author Unknown. 1999. State Heritage Report [internet]. Australia: National Trust of Australia; [cited 2007 Jul 24]. 7 p. Available from: http://www.ntwa.com.au/heritage/convention99-workshops.shtml

Author Unknown. 2006. Kennewick Man in Time. *ACPAC Newsletter* April 2006: 1.

Author Unknown. 2006. Interior Secretary Kempthorne Appoints New Member to NAGPRA. Native American Times 12(45):1.

Author Unknown. 2006. Tribes to repatriate remains of 143 individuals, 6,200 artifacts. *Confederated Umatilla Journal* 9(3):1.

Author Unknown. Native Earthworks Society. 2006 Feb 17. For Your Information [personal e-mail]. Accessed 2006 Feb 17.

Author Unknown. 2006. Wider View [internet]. Harleysville (PA): Mennonite Heritage Center; [cited 2007 Jul 27]. 3 p. Available from: http://www.thirdway.com/wv/?ID=463Author Unknown. 2007. NAGPRA meeting planned to organize regional coalition among local tribes. *Native American Times* 13(12):3.

Author Unknown. 2007. Remains, objects to be reburied. *Confederated Umatilla Journal* 10(6):1-2.

Author Unknown. Native American Reburial [Internet]. The Christian Century; [cited 2007 Jul 23]. 1 p. Available from: http://search.atlaonline.com/pls/eli/ashow?aid= ATLA0000830949.

Author Unknown.. Frequently Asked Questions [internet]. Washington D.C., Repatriation Office; [cited 2007 Jul 12]. 4 p. Available from: http://www.nmnh.si.edu/anthro/repatriation/faq/index.htm

Author Unknown. Native American Graves Protection and Repatriation Act (NAGPRA) [internet]. Flagstaff (AZ): Northern Arizona University; [cited 2007 Aug 15]. 2 p. Available from: http://www.nau.edu/-hcpo-o/current/nagpratx.htm

Author Unknown. 2007. *Native American Graves Protection and Repatriation Act Compliance Specialists* [internet]. Bernstein & Associates; [cited 2007 Jul 12]. 4 p. Available from: http://www.nagpra.biz/wst_page 4.html.

Author Unknown. 2007. Remains, objects to be reburied. *Confederated Umatilla Journal* 10(6):1-2.

Author Unknown. Native American Reburial [Internet]. The Christian Century; [cited 2007 Jul 23]. 1 p. Available from: http://search.atlaonline.com/pls/eli/ashow?aid= ATLA0000830949.

Author Unknown. Native American Sacred Lands Act [internet]. Sacred Land; [cited 2007 Jul 13]. 7 p. Available from: http://www.sacredland.org/legal_pages/NA_SLA_HR_.html.

Author Unknown. The Prehistoric Native American Collections [internet]. Albuquerque (NM): Laboratory of Human Osteology: Maxwell Museum of Anthropology; [cited 2007 Jul 12]. 1 p. Available from: http://www.unm.edu/-osteolab/coll_pre.html.

Author Unknown. Prehistory's Future – Will Politics Bury Science? [internet]. Friends of America's Past; [cited 2007 Jul 12]. 3 p. Available from: http://www.friendsofpast.org/earliest-americans/031228SL.html.

Author Unknown. Repatriations: Cayuga Nation of New York [internet]. Philadelphia (PA): Penn Museum; [cited 2007 Jul 12]. 1 p. Available from: http://www.museum.upenn.edu/new/exhibits/nagpra/cayuga.shtml

Author Unknown. Repatriations: Chugach Alaska Corporation [Internet]. Philadelphia (PA): Penn Museum; [cited 2007 Jul 12]. 1 p. Available from: http://www.museum.upenn.edu/new/exhibits/nagpra/chugach.shtml

INDEX

D

E

F

G